My Summer in Hollywood

This is my summer in Hollywood

Mark R Luberto

ISBN 978-93-5667-287-1
© Mark R Luberto 2022
Published in India 2022 by Pencil

Contributors:
Illustrator: Lydia Hines Luberto

A brand of
One Point Six Technologies Pvt. Ltd.
123, Building J2, Shram Seva Premises,
Wadala Truck Terminal, Wadala (E)
Mumbai 400037, Maharashtra, INDIA
E connect@thepencilapp.com
W www.thepencilapp.com

Author biography

Mark R Luberto is a blogger, writing and recording for Luvispros Guitar Podcast on Anchor.fm. He has a Certificate in the guitar from Musicians Institute, and has spent the last 25 years playing everything from blues and jazz to rock and metal. When I'm not combining my passion for writing and producing music, I'm a technician during the day. Mark records for a number of bands and his indie record label Swamp Muck Records
I was Born back in the 1960's and raised in New Jersey

But after Living and peforming in Memphis with the band My-Rage He became the guitarist known as " Luvis ".

Before my summer of 1988, I was a teenager going to high school taking music lessons from friends.

After my summer in California, I became obsessed with every kind of music on this planet and decided to always learn more, play more and teach more. My philosophy is " Music Means Freedom ".

Its been a long strange trip so lets jam.

CONTENTS

Epigraph

*" There are eight things that will change your life and they are*C D E F G A B C "

Foreword

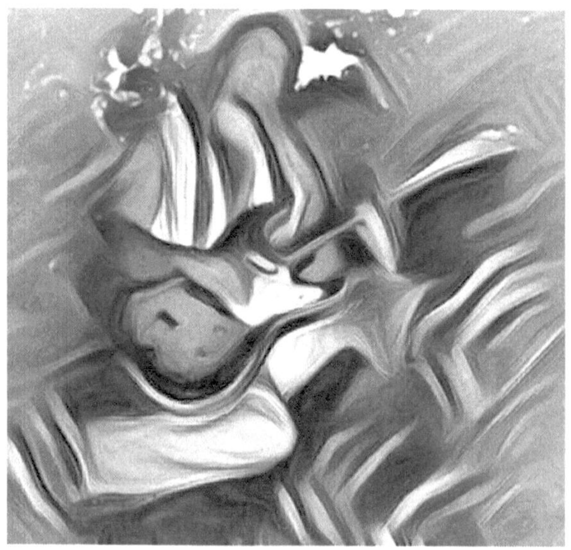

It was a time when music was all about wild guitar solos, slap bass, drum solos, long hair and forming a band in California.

Check out the songs that helped me through the this summer of 1988

on my Spotify channel

1988 Musicians Institute Summer Jams .

Thank You

Preface

I was 19 yrs old and I wanted to spend my summer in California going to a Music School called Musicians Institute. These are those stories that I remember from that famous summer in Hollywood 1988.

Acknowledgements

This book is dedicated to my Mom
RIP Marietta Thersa Nasco Luberto.
My mom loved to sing and she always listened to my crazy songs I recorded. She pushed me to go to music school and she was awesome.
Luv Ya and " I'm a Tomato "

Chapter 1 - Major & Minor Scales

May / June 1st 1988

Hello Hollywood !!!!!! I am now a resident of this city. I live in a 3-story apartment building, about a 5-minute walk from Musicians Institute. I have no job yet but I'm looking everywhere for something cool that will pay me some fast cash. I haven't made any friends yet but I've only been here a few days. I have this big binder of lessons, sheet music and tablature to read and learn. School is very intense and all the teachers are monsters at playing guitar at GIT aka the Guitar Institute of Technology. I feel so good to be at the school. I have even applied for a job at Musicians Institute, working at the players supply store atter hours. There has to be over 500 students at the school right now.

I got to meet the creators of this great school today Mr Pat and Mr Bruce who are both monster jazz players. Class starts about 6:00 pm monday thru thursday. The school is open all day for us to learn anything we want using video lesson and one on one training sessions. The rehearsal room is open after 12:00. Fridays and Saturdays are for performing. Sundays are for private lessons. I called my Mom today back in home and asked for her advice on life and told her " Thank God for Hollywood, Do I sound like a Cali boy yet ".

It's nice to hear a friendly voice and people who love me. The trip so far has been kinda crazy and as soon as I got to this city I almost got into a fight all over my leather jacket. I'm not far from a cool pawn shop and I'll be picking up a 10 speed bike so I don't have to drive around wasting gas.

The Buick Regal is still alive and driving ok but needs and oil change, but the car made it all the way from New Jersey with minor problems along the way thank god. It took me 5 days to drive out here and that was only because I went off course and hit some adventure spots and I'm sure glad I did. I have now seen the heartland, the mountains, the desert, city life and the now the pacific ocean. Like Wow man.

I spent my 1st day driving to the PA/Ohio boarder and staying at a koa camp ground. Pitching a mean green 2 man camping tent. Made a fire and watched fireworks because it was Memorial day. Some guy in an RV talked my ear off about taking Rt70 instead of Rt80. His motor home was brand new, he told me I could " stay with him in the RV there's plenty of room ". I drank a beer with him thanked him for his kindness and fell asleep in my cozy tent.

I woke up being eaten by mosquitoes in the middle of the night. It was boiling hot out and I didnt get any sleep. Woke up kinda mad at life at 6:00am packed up and left without taking a free hot shower. Drove all day without any road construction into Indiana, Illinois and Iowa where I pulled over into a rest area and went to the bathroom. I rolled up a doobie and smoked it walking around the parking lot. I headed down the road and within 2 seconds from the rest area I got pulled over for speeding 70 in a 55. It was the fastest speeding ticket I ever got in my life. I think the trooper was younger than me. Pulled into a truck stop later that night and I parked on the wrong side of the lot. Some truckers got pissed and woke me up. Some guy with a baseball bat told me I wasn't allowed to be there. I started my car and peeled out. Left them all with my horn blasting and me yelling " Fuck You ".

I had to sleep in my car down the road at another truck stop. Woke up hot , sweaty and cramped with the sun in my eyes at 5:00 am. This is not fun at all so far on the road and I hope it gets better.

I Hit the road hard on my 3rd day to make some time but had car trouble when my passenger side rear tire started to bubble up. I spent about 3hrs trying to get somebody to fix it. Holy cow the flies in Kansas are everywhere and in packs flying around me inside and outside my car. After getting another tire and fixing my spare tire I left to get some food at a Stuckeys. I ordered a Cheeseburger and fries. I went to the other side of the store and bought some gas and beer. I walked back and sat down at the table waiting for my food. I opened my cold beer and started drinking it. Immediately the manager at stuckeys yelled at me telling me " You can't drink alcohol in the restaurant."

Then he asked me " Are you even 21 "
I told him " keep your food I'm outa here " and walked to my car and drove to the highway where I drove like a bat outa hell. I Drove till midnight where I slept at a truck stop in Kansas city. I didn't get any sleep and I wished I had a tarp for the car. I woke up in the car and hauled ass into Nebraska and Oklahoma where I bought a nice fishing pole set at a little roadside souvenir shop. I pulled into Colorado and had breakfest at some roadside diner. I was about an 1hr from Denver and found a KOA campground and pitched my tent. Went into town bought some hot dogs to cook on the fire later. Drove back to the camp ground and found out a storm was coming through and I was gonna have to get to higher ground so I got my money back. The campground owners told me to go to a hotel down the road to be safe. I'm glad I listened to them cause it was tornado like conditions. Some of the worst rain storms I had ever seen. Spent the night watching TV playing guitar in a hotel room watching the pouring rain. Being a road dog is a tough life .

The past couple of days have been really wild as I'm trying to get used to being in Hollywood. I have been to the ocean and the Santa Monica pier. I am lilly white and don't look like I'm from L.A at all - hahaha
I'm here and its wonderful. I'm California dreaming in real time. To have a real bed and a place to shower is great. I picked up a nice blue 10 speed Huffy from the pawn shop for $80 and drove down to the tattoo shop and got my name MARK with a red anarchy symbol.
The nice lady who tattoo'd it would tell me "the red will fade ". When I walked out the door with my new skin art someone had knifed my tire. I pushed my bike back to the

trusty car where all my tools are setup. This week has been fast and I'm happy to be here in Lost Angeles.

This place is awesome on so many levels. I bike ride all over these streets during the day with my acoustic strapped to my back. I sit at the steps outside MI jamming acoustic guitar almost everyday. Sipping beer in my brown paper bag taking puffs. Lots of firsts are what this whole adventure is really about. I have been playing guitar every single day. I wake up and play guitar to get my hands warmed up and than I run through a bunch of scales like the pentatonic, the whole tone and chromatics. I like playing the dorian and aeolian modes plus I like the mixolydian scale. I can whip out two hand tapping and my classical picking is pretty good. I need help with learning how to read sheet music really fast like those LA Studio Session cats I keep hearing about. I didn't know there was going to be all these great side stories from the teachers. Everybody is in the loop with the past sessions and studios with the record business and the film business.

One of my classmates is a California kid name Tommy who plays a bright blue strat in class. He just got a side gig working with Hanna Barbara studios, but he hopes to go full time to MI in the future. Another guy in my class is from the San Francisco area name Joseph who uses a Gibson acoustic. He digs the Grateful Dead and wants to play more blue rock music and join a band. There's about 25 of us in this class and two more classs down the hall for guitars and the same for drums and bass. The place is air conditioned and sound proof. We each get our own personal area to play, with music stand, no amp, lots of mirrors, and we can drink soft drinks. No smoking unless were outside on the balcony. The Instructors all say " Dont be scared to ask questions and help the person next to you if you can ".

The luck of the Irish I must have for I have an interview for a sales job tomorrow at 10 out in Santa Monica according to the front desk guy at my hotel. I'm on my way up. I have to carry my blue 10 speed up 3 flights of steps along with my guitar stuff it can be a real pain in the ass. I think I'm the only guy from the east coast living in this building. I wish I had a refrigerator and a stove. My apartment is so small, the apartment is on the 3rd floor.

My window face's Hollywood boulvard . I can open the window and look down the street but there's nothing to look at. it really kinda sucks but its mine all mine. It hasn't rained since that crazy night in Denver . I really miss the trip across the United States. I hope my pictures came out ok. I look around my room for clothes to wear for tomorrows job interview. The map for LA is my life blood and I use it for everything. The names to some of these streets are wild. I have seen them only in movies and in books. Hollywood looks better at night. It looks just like those old black and white movies. Famous people are out here and so am I. Running low on cash is a giant worry me out here. I want to buy this Black BC Rich guitar thats at the pawn shop. Everybody loves my guitar and I'm the only guy with one. I went to town with stickers in NYC right before I moved here and plastered the guitar with all of them. I also might be the only one who bought both an acoustic and electric which is perfect for everything we do.

Good morning you west coast day dreamers. Today is June Nineteenth and I am going to my private lesson today at MI/GIT. My instructor is a Full time MI student who plays a bright White Strat. She's a monster at playing and can shred that guitar. She's showing me how to read sheet music. She has some great techniques for sight-reading. Her name is Jenifer and she plays in a jazz band.

They perform at the local coffee shops on the weekend. They have open mic's and so I might have to check it out. Almost every teacher has a gig somewhere in this city. All we have to do is show our MI/GIT ID card and we either get in free or its half price. The momma and the poppa's California Dreaming song is playing in the back ground on my radio. It reminds me of my Mom driving in her mean green Mustang down the highway. I always thought my Mom had a great singing voice.

The sun is super bright today and I'm going for a early morning bike ride to the beach. I have to call NJ and wish my Dad a Happy Father's Day. I have to go the laundry mat to wash some clothes today. I picked up the latest edition of Conan the Barbarian comic and " My Crom " Its savage to read.

The LA sky is bright blue with no clouds in sight. Last night on the Sunset Strip hanging out was a lot of Fun.

I ran around those streets talking to every girl I could. I almost jumped into a car with 2 girls heading to Venice beach but I didnt know where to ditch the bike and they took off faster than a green light at the drag strip. I am all over Hollywood and It's been great to see all these little stores. My favorite is the army surplus store. With the knifes and gas masks along with camo jackets and jet black military boots. Patches, posters and amazing manuals and books I can be in here all day. I ask to fill out an application and the guy says

" we dont take applications here, you ever been in the service ". I looked at him laughing " No but I signed up for selective service does that count ". He said no and walked away and I walked out looking for another job.

The town of Hollywood is filled with lots of No's. Like I didn't know you can't walk across the street like in NYC. I crossed the street to go to Mc Donalds and a Chips Cop drove up and almost ran me over. I was givin a ticket for Jay Walking. The cop yelled at me like i murdered somebody "We dont walk across busy streets WE USE THE CROSSWALKS IN THIS CITY ".

I gave the nice officer my drivers id and he gave me a ticket. This is way to funny man.

Monday morning June 20, 1988

The sun shines bright this morning and I'm happy to be here. I have to drive to my 1st interview in Santa Monica. I roll my windows down and head out of Hollywierd driving down the Sunset Strip in the fast lane. I flip on the radio and Winger plays on the radio " She's only 17 ".

As I pull up to this all white building for my sales job I can see that I'm not the only one here for this job. About 7 people walk in, and we are all told to fill out an application. Without an explanation as to what the job is, some guy in a suit asks me if that's my car outside. I'm asked to park in the back of the building. After moving my car I come back and everybody is in a room listening to a guy talk about Sales. After 15 minutes of being prepped for sales he walks out the product we are to sell books, cook books, encyclopedias, self-help books and kids books. I'm not happy and of course almost everybody gets up and walks to the door. I'm walking away when I'm told " Hey Mark wait a second " I walk into his office " This is Jimmy he's our top salesman and if you want he can teach you the ropes. Your Gauaranteed $300 the 1st week " . Jimmy's a nice guy with a nice dull brown suit. He's about 10 yrs older than me with a wife and kid. He tells me he has the best routes in a great business district "If you have a car we can load up some books and samples in your car and drop them off".

We drove out to Glendale and spent the rest of the day walking in and out of businesses dropping off our samples. We ate at an IN n OUT burger place. Jimmy lost his drivers licence for DUI and is going through a divorce with his wife. He's a quiet guy and is real focused on selling books for this company. He swears by it but I kinda feel bad for the guy. He spoke of his kids and showed me some pictures of the family. I can tell this job isn't going to work out, But I need $300. Friday can't come fast enough.

It's kinda nice to drive around California cause I don't know where I am. I'm just going with the flow.

Today is June 22nd.

I wake up with a summer ear-ache just like I did back in NJ swimming at the lake. I must have some of the pacific ocean still in my ears. I am working today as a salesman but I really just feel like the designated driver. I filled out another couple of applications at a print shop in Hollywood and Santa Monica. I think I'd rather be printing than selling books. It all fun and games till fridays 1st paycheck. The sun shines bright and there's "no rain in sight" say's the weather man on my new favorite radio station Knac.

Night Moves plays in the background as we drive into South Pasadena today and drop off these orders of books at some warehouse. We stop at a MCD for some breakfast and I strike a conversation with 2 blonde sisters from around the LA area. I ask for her number and I tell her I'll call her later. This is my 1st telephone number to have some California fun. Jimmy tells me to be careful and be a little more professional while out and about since we represent the company. I'm starting to think Jimmy is wimpy and we dont talk until lunchtime. Jimmy loved to look over his paperwork as if its some bible with hidden message's.

We got a short day and so I drop him off in Santa Monica at the end and I spend some time playing guitar down on the beach. There's lots of people today at the beach and I prop myself not to far from 2 California babes in bikinis. This is a young mans dream life. The fishermen are next to the pier line up with all kinds of fishing setups. Seagulls circle over me and I am doing just fine as frog hair split 3 ways. I open up my knapsack and pull out the GIT book to see what my lessons are for tonight .

Chapter 2 - Nobody's Your Friend
On Payday

June 23 1988

Tonight is going to be awesome I can't wait. I'm doing great at school and I met some cool dudes yesterday at school while I was playing guitar at my car. Larry and Damian are from Hawaii and have a band that plays AC/DC covers . The band is called " Loud and Proud ". Larry plays a Gibson SG just like Angus Young. Damian the drummer and plays a jet black Tama 5 piece. They live in the Hollywood Hills not to far from the school. I tell them about a pizza place that serves alcohol. Larry and Damian are huge stoners and ask me if I can get any herb in town since they smoked all there Maui bud a few days ago. We instantly become friends and off we drive to my apartment to get some smoke. Damian sits in the back seat and says "Hey bruh you drove this car across the country cause old Betsy seems to seen better days ". From this moment on the buick regal of love now becomes old Betsy. Shocked and in awe of my shitty looking little apartment these guys feel for my life. I tell them about the fight I had last weekend with the boyfriend to the girl on the 2nd floor who walked home with me from the grocery store. She was asking about my car and driving all the way from NJ.

We walked and talked until we got to the front of the building and than the door flew open and this heavy set drunk guy starts yelling at the girl then trys to punch me in the face and missed. I walked to my apartment and listened to the yelling all night long. I tell them that " we are all friends now and Jose is my friend who looks out for me and my car but it was a crazy night ", but in the back of my head you just never know.

I seem to keep these guys amused with my stories and they think the place I stay at is a real dump. Larry says I can stay at their apartment if things ever get crazy at my place. Larry asks me if I can get cigarettes for him at the gas station. I tell him " This guy at this gas station loves me. He sells me anything like beer, wine and cigarettes its fucking great ". Larry and Damian are both 17 and this is there first time away from home. Larry's parents are divorced and his Dad lives in Hawaii and His Mom lives in Anaheim. Damian entire family is polynesian, and he was born in Maui. Damian like to write his name as Ha-Y-N on all this stuff and Larry only wears AC-DC t shirts.

We roll up our first joint together and drive down Hollywood blvd toward the pizza spot. This would become our favorite little spot for the next few months. I order a pitcher of beer and a pepperoni extra cheese pizza. Larry leans over and says " They aren't going to ID you brah " .

I was told that all MI students get 10 % off the bill. There only about 6 people in the whole restaurant. We devour that pizza in minutes and slam the pitcher of beer. " Hey you guys want to go to the beach ".

Twenty minutes later were at the boardwalk in Santa Monica laughing at the ocean. They hadn't seen it yet and so my work here is done.

Today is Tuesday and it's a hot one here in downtown Santa Monica. Old betsy is doing well in this heat as long as the windows are down. We all have class's at GIT and PIT tonight and my favorite guitarist is the one and only Mr Nick who teaches us Electric guitar and Mr Jamie who teaches us music theory. Both teachers are amazing at playing guitar. Nicks band is playing in a few weeks and wants us all to show up and support him. Nick loves to play these amazing sweep picking two hand tapping tricks. Jamie on the other hand is so melodic and super smooth I want to play like him someday. All the teachers are super badass on the fretboard and with the business side of things.This Thursdays seminar is with a guy name Paul Hanson. I have seen him in the Guitar Player Mags. Should be a cool event. Last night was a crazy night with Mr Chas on Chords and Rythem and Mr Storming Norman on ear training sight reading. Both teachers are intense with monster chops and tons of knowledge about the fret board. Wensdays are Mr Jamie playing Acoustic

Guitar and Mr Jimmy on Single String techniques.Thursdays are Concerts and Seminars with Mr Bruce or Mr Steve. Friday and Saturdays are our personal days to perform and go to a show, rehearsals, recording sessions. Sunday's are our private instructors and jam sessions with Mr Steve . Now I'm kinda curious what teachers Larry has. Larry said that I'm in the class with all the pretty girls. I think he's "correct amondo". We got a girl in my class that looks like Lita Ford .Another girl that looks like Pat Benitar and a one girl who looks like the ultimate hippie chick from Woodstock whose name is Angel. I'm a very very very lucky boy . I have gone through my GIT book forwards and backwards and so has every other classmate. The sight reading and the music thoery is so interesting. There's a ton of cool stuff in this book. Everybody is trying to play arpeggios and sweep picking. We all are looking to start a band. It nice to live with a drummer and be in a band together .Everybody walks around with their guitar sling to their shoulder like it's normal. We past each other as if its no big deal. The halls look like a sea of bass players drummers and guitarist all walking in single file to our classes. Its very funny to see so many musicians in one place. Strings pop and picks break every other minute. Guitar cords are always being lost and only 1 kid in class records the sessions on a micro tape recorder. My favorite guy at GIT is my buddy Ronnie James otherwise known as DIO. I swear to god dude looks like Ronnie James Dio and he's a ripper on the guitar like Ingwie or Vai all mixed into one fret board. Dudes a monster and I really enjoying watching him play . I saw him the other day, and we Instantly started jamming some Crazy fast guitar parts. He Loves to solo, he will solo to anything , anytime, any week, anywhere. I love this Guy.

It's the 29th of June
I swear to god it has not rained since I've been here. It was boiling hot out today. Big blue skies for miles and it seemed like all the girls are wearing barely anything out here in Santa Monica. I'm in a constant transition and its all happening so fast I don't know how else to live, but to just Rock and Roll. Hahahah its all major scales baby doll like do re mi fa so la ti do. I'm now living in a new spot up the street off the main ave. I'm working at a new place and I'm in a new LA Band called Loud and Proud. We are a AC/DC tribute band and it's been a blast to get in the rehearsal room and blast out one of my favorite guitarists Angus Young. My 1st album was Dirty Deeds Done Dirt Cheap and than came High Voltage. Black in Black came out when I was in Middle school and I almost got to see the
" For those about to rock " tour with crazy Keithly and " How does it feel to want " Nick . But I didn't go cause I had no money and I think those guys might have killed me. hahahaha . Loud and Proud is an awesome band to be a part of and I think its fate that we all met in Hollywood. Larry plays all the Angus parts and I play the Malcolm parts. Damian calls me Malks and so is everybody else. " Yo Malks " is all I've been hearing and it's been pretty funny. We are the 3 Stooges of Rock and Roll over here. I quit my job as a book salesman and they all were very upset. I got a Print shop job working at the Copy Kat print shop in Santa Monica. Its Just 4 or 5 blocks from the beach. That's a huge plus cause I want to live over here. I have my lunch on the boardwalk and it's so busy with

tourists over here. I fit right in with the crew and have made another new friend named Jose. He works in bindery department and lives with his sister a few miles away. I moved out of the motel and now stay at off Yucca street and Beechwood ave called the Beechwood Villas. I'm like a stow away over here cause the lease only says 2 people. I dont have a key yet but I can park my car in the under ground car garage. Very cool since I keep getting parking tickets every week that I've been here.

This weekend is a 1st for so many reasons and it's all just fun fun. I am doing well at school and i'm practing everything on these pages of my GIT summer schedule. It been real intense. Lots of hands on training. The teachers are so helpful and kind. They all make sure we all understand the concepts, the style and how to improvise with the material. Tonights class is acoustic guitar class with Mr Jamie and Single String class with Mr Jimmy. Both class's are fast paced with lots of info and tons of sheet music to read. I try to keep up and just get lost in it all at times. The days are slow at work and nights are super fast at school. I miss being alone and not answering everybody questions all the time. We have been drinking every night since I moved in with these guys. Trying out new beers and whiskeys has been a goal. We got pretty drunk on Maddog 20/20 and we got really drunk on Soco shots aka Southern Comfort. Being able to buy alcohol has been a real cool thing and I keep getting new bottles to try every other day. Larry loves his Marboros red and High Lifes. Damian loves the Camels with Budweisers. We all enjoy the Hustler, Swank and the Penthouse Mags. Ha-ha hahaa. This weekend is the 4th of July and it will be my first 4th of July without family from NJ. We have been invited to

Larrys moms house for a party.

I have Fireworks that I bought in Ohio. I'm trying to whip us up a rock show but larrys mom might not be down with all the loud music. She lives in a really nice section of Anaheim and she's a real estate agent. " She's kinda Uptight " says Larry.

I like to call Larry "Lee" sometimes and of course Lee has a Sister and she will be stoping over tomorrow night. Ha-y-n says Lee's sister is a mess and kinda ugly so I probadly won't like her. She "Real Stuck up at times". Larry of course agrees and we all laugh at how we all have the same things in common. I am so glad I met these guys and I hope we can get over to the school soon and start recording our jams.

June 30th 1988

Its National Corvette day. I woke up on the couch at the love shack and it felt great to be in central AC. The whole apartment is pretty nice and clean. I am amazed that my new band mates are living so High on the Hog. I was stuck on the blvd of broken dreams and now I'm living in the Hollywood hills like a punk rocker who won the lottery. The new job is so easy breezy for me and I'm having fun printing one and two color letters heads and envelopes on a AB Dick 360 printing press. I wish the guys back in Morristown NJ could see me. I miss my old job and all my friends back there. We had some crazy cool fun playing guitar and learning all those Grateful Dead songs. Printing is a cool trade and i'm so thankful to have a skilled trade to fall back on cause I dont want to be a ditch digger or street sweeper just yet.Today was special day of seminars at the school and I can't believe I got to see Vinny Moore. Mr

Steve introduced him to our class of students maybe 60 students listening to his new album. He basically played along to himself using a 4 track recorder in a PA. Either or he was killing it with his sweep picking and arpeggio techniques. I really enjoyed watching him play his music. I was able to see how contained and caged his hands always were on the fret board. He would play his blue Jackson guitar type with a slow downward right hand while sliding and rolling his fingers up and down those strings. I don't think anybody left there not trying to play like him. I sat next to Dio, and he kept saying " I can do that ". After our seminar we all walked over to the rehearsal area and tried to play the sheet music to Mr Moore work sheets. It became a giant hangout, and we eventually started to play the basic jams like Judas Priest, the Ramones and Motorhead. Lee and Damian finally showed up, and we got into our ACDC Highway to Hell /Hells Bells extended long set with drum solo . We had prolonged our time slot at school and so we decided to head over to the pizza joint to get a pitcher and a slice. One More day till we all head over to Orange county for our 1st 4th of July in California. Its loud and proud's 1st real gig. Lee said we could bring the gear over and setup in the back yard. This is gonna be so cool. I'm looking forward to getting outta holly weird for a hot minute. I got some smoke, fireworks and a bottle of Jim Beam to bring along. Tomorrow is payday and " Nobody is your friend on payday " . I'm looking forward to getting my last paycheck from the old sales job and I'm gonna get a fresh paycheck from the print shop. I should be good for this weekend.This whole week is so wild with crazy new job stuff and wild guitar lessons. I feel refreshed from all the past issues.

I drove here to find a band and play guitar. That what i'm doing every single day out here. It seems so right. I was born for this life style. Lots of gigs this weekend from all our teachers. Everybody is doing something cool. Lots of people are going to observatory parking lot for the fireworks. I've been planing this 4th of July event since May and I love fireworks. I am thinking about getting business cards made with my guitar lesson info on one side and The Loud and Proud band info on the other side. It would be nice to make up some cool flyers and posters for our future shows and gigs. It seems that every single teacher has their own custom logo to identify themselves. It a thing with these guys. Upside down letters or numbers. Guitar picks with their name in it. Horses pulling carriages backwards. Stuff like that. I'm thinking a big Marijuana leaf and a beer bottle " Loud and Proud " LA's best stoner band playing everything from AC/DC to Cheech and Chong hahahahahaha. We walked out that Pizzeria tonight a little bit tipsy. The 3 of us are laughing at everything we saw at school today. people walk outa our way. We are Loud and Proud on these city streets and thats no lie. We get back to old betsy and she starts up without fail. Peeling out is easy and off we go down Hollywood ave and up to Yucca street past Capitol Records. " We need to get our music into the hands of and AnR man at Capital before we leave this place " "That's our goal" "Who's got a 4 track we can use" "we should record a couple of covers and a couple of originals" " we need to practice" " dude you past our street you needed to turn left " ha ha ha.

Chapter 3 - Arpeggios and Sweep Picking

Friday July 1st 1988

I wake up with the sun in my eyes again and its exciting. It's about 6am and I'm completely wasted from last night's shots, beers and poker game. I wake up to take a nice hot shower. I turn the light switch on and it's only the black light. Everything is glowing light blue and when you close the door a giant poster of Led Zep glows .

So I grab my sunshades and jump into the shower. The light blue haze against the bathroom wall makes me feel better. I look at the toilet tank and see a beer from last night that Lee probably left in here. I grab that can and tilt my head back and finish the can. Good Morning Los Angeles. I hope that beer wasn't a prank.

This rock and roll life man is free and easy. I start to remember things that i said and realized I promised to pay these guys $150 a week to live here starting tomorrow I mean Today. Fuck me running . It's now 6:16 am and I have to be at work in 39 minutes today. Tonights gonna be a great friday night in LA. I don't care what anybody says. I'm living in the Hollywood Hills now. I'm gonna bike up to that Hollywood sign one of these days. I sneak out the house to the car and load up my stuff. I wish I could bike to work but it's just to damn far and i'm already running late.

Old betsy starts up and roars down the street. Its another wicked early morning in the city. The bus zips by picking up the locals. The taxis are all lines up in front of Mc Donalds. Bag ladys sift the garbage bins. The homeless person begging for some change. I order some food at the drive thru and smash my breakfast, while one arm swings out the window of the car driving down the road.

I drive down Sunset and It's the best place to be right now. Business owners are sweeping the front steps. Tons of street people are getting ready for there day. I am lucky to be able to drive around this city. I get in the parking lot and pull into a parking spot. I notice my co-worker Jose and start to talk to him about the Los Angeles Dodgers game last night. He doesn't like the Dodgers he's a Padres fan.

I'm not at my printing press and the owner Mike says to us " You guys are late " he's pissed off. 20 minutes into my shift and the boss shows me some letterheads that didnt get sent to the customer because of a spelling error. " You printed these and there not correct, why didnt you proof read your work ".

This is not how I want to spend my morning. I feel like crap knowing my boss is pissed off at me. It's gonna be one of those days. Thank god its Friday today and like Jimmy crack corn says " I Don't Care ". I'm chilling like Dylan and I'm Audi 5000 from that stupid print shop at 4:30

This weekend is gonna be awesome in Anaheim and I can't wait to jam. The Loud and Proud band has been getting better and better and its all thanks to the great teachers at GIT. Larry and I have been teaching each other what we have learned and what we both know is that we both have our own style. Lee is learning how to two hand tap for the first time. I try to get that sweep picking technique. We both need to lower our amps when we play in the rehearsal studio. We get to use these Peavey combo amps and we blast those amps. Its kinda hard to hear each other at times. Damian thinks we need to be Louder. He pounds on those drums when were playing Hells Bells or anything for that Matter. I tell everybody that I meet, about the band I'm playing in. When I'm at the print shop I tell everybody about the band. The only cool guy there is Jose. I had to drop him off at his house down on the East side of LA today. I met his Sister and her name is Alessandra. She seems kinda like a wild thang.

We smoked a little bit of herb that I had and she told me she's got a great connection. Jose wants to hang out soon and show me around California. Alexandra asks me if the car will make to Tijuana for the weekend. We could all go there for only $100 bucks. " Its double the amount in American cash " she keeps saying . We can drink, smoke, eat and " party like Cholo's ". She speaks with such a heavy twists of words that I don't know about yet. It's like

Damian and Larry when they start talking in Pigeon ."I'm a Howlie Boy" and I'm a "Gringo" all in the span of just four weeks.

I am in love with all the different ways people talk out here. I really dig my new nickname " MALKS ". I agree to go to Tijuana in the future with them but not this weekend and off I go to Betsy for that long ride back to Hollywood. I get back to the Hollywood Hills and park old Betsy inside the garage. I'm so excited and also very tired. I grab my work clothes and favorite coffee cup and start to walk across to the big gray door that opens to a carpeted hallway to the 1st floor. I walk up to the door and its not locked. I have been sneak attacking these guys for the past couple of days. I'm like Inspector Clueso waiting for Kato to attack me or vice versa. I have snuck in and scared these fools twice now. Slowly I twist the door open and walk inside. Nobody's here. It's an empty vessel of a room that I get to walk freely about. Its nice to be here all alone.

I open the fridge grab a cold Heineken out the crisper. I get in the shower and take me a nice hot shower. I jump out and walk the apartment naked to my wardrobe closet and find some clothes. The radio is blasting out The Who's Pinball Wizard on Knac 105.5 LA's hardest rock station. I turn on my little amp and plug in my 9 volt to the MXR distortion pedal. I find a pick and hit that barred E chord and press the DOD delay pedal and listen for the fade out. I open the GIT book to the electric guitar section and look at the notes to the arpeggios patterns and start to jam out to the radio.

The door suddenly flys open and its Damian and Larry " Malks where ya been Man, we went Swimming and that was so Refreshing". " We have a swimming pool here ? "

Hahahaha "Ya man but your not on the lease, and we only have 2 pool pass's so your kinda outta luck bruh ". That's some bullshit but I'm ok with it I guess. These guys are gonna take forever to get ready to go out to see this jazz show my teacher Mr Chas is doing tonight.

I decide to go for a bike ride and get some pizza and check out what happening on the Ave. "Malks do you have that $150 for rent this week I'm thinking of getting some us some real good food and these sweet ass cowboy boots for the 4th of July show". I reach into my duffel bag and grab out $150 bucks and hand it to him. " Malks this great brah thanks ". Lee looks at me and we both give each other the stink eye. I leave for the pizza joint on the blue bike of love. The sun is hanging over me every pedal I take. I cruise down Beechwood to Yucca st and cruise over to Wilshire blvd and past my old apartment building.

I pedal past the pawn shop and past the liquor store. I get up Hollywood and Cherokee. I look over to my right and nobody is in the parking lots but I notice 2 guys from GIT that I was talking to the other day.

Its Dee and Tommy (Dee looks like Twisted Sister and Tommy looks like he's in Motley Crew) getting out of this blue Toyota pickup truck with a set of drums. We talk for a minute about School stuff and they tell me they live here. I get invited inside to this Massive three bedroom apartment/condo with the kitchen window look over the entire parking lot. We sit in the kitchen and smoke some killer bud while talking life and about each other. Dee's from Pittsburgh and is a radio dj who came to this music school in Hollywood for drums . The percussion institute of technology aka PIT as we call it. He's got long blonde curly hair and has a love of getting autographs from famous people. He pulls out a black book with names like Iggy Pop, Alice Cooper and Joey Ramone. Dee says " I've met a lot of famous bands and people while working at the radio station. I carry this book with me everywhere and ask them to sign it. I even got Vinnie Moores autograph last week. I'm trying to get everybodys name from that school. Tommy is from Las Vegas and he's a drummer in a rock band back there. He's been playing drums for a few years and always wanted to go to Musicians Institute. These guys are cool and so is this place they live in.

They've got a killer kenwood stereo system with a nice dual cassette player. "We record from time to time using my dual decks to mix it all down to one track ". Dee says " We should all get together and play some songs and hit the road touring all over America ". I tell them I live over by the Capitol Records buiding and I'm always trying to talk to the security guys about talking to the AnR department about my killer local band. They dont know where the building is and dont drive around LA all that much. We decide to start collaborating on music and having a jam over the weekend. Simple Man plays on the radio in the background of the kitchen. Two drum sets are in the living room setup side by side . Tommys got the jet black Tama 5 piece and Dee has the dark blue Pearl set. A red light hangs from the ceiling. Posters of Led Zep and Ozzy hang on the wall. Incense burns the herbal smell away and I tell these guys I'm off to the pizza joint for some slices of cheese.

July 2nd, 3rd, 4th 1988
The radio plays " American Pie " and than Cheap Tricks " I want you to want Me " on the radio. Old betsy is being loaded up with all the drum gear and guitar amps. How

quickly the car isn't that big anymore. Lee says to Damain " We all might have to sit in the front seat and I'm not sitting next to Malks ". Saturday was another blue sky rain free hot summer day.

I changed the oil in the car and air'd up the tires. Put some water in the radiator and so the car is all ready to go. Damian and Lee went to the store on the strip and bought some real Hawaiian kona coffee, real bread and these killer red and black cowboy boots. They were so happy to finally have some cash . I was the only one who worked a day job. These guys sleep all day and go to school at night, thats really about it for them. I also get to see the city more and my driving skills navigating through the city is getting a whole lot better. The big news on the Musicians Institute free bill board is all the upcoming seminars and concerts with Tommy Tedesco, Joe Pass and Paul Gilbert. The Monsters of Rock tour is happening and so is the band Slayer.

I have to save up for these concerts. Both of these guys have never seen any of them. The past 30 days have been super crazy in Hollywood. We are all excited to go on tour this weekend. Lee and I get guitar strings and new picks from the players supply store at school. I try to get Dee and Tommy to show up, but they are going to Vegas for the 4th of July.

We need to get out of Hollywood and I cant wait to see more of California .

The sky is hazy shade of clouds but no rain on the forecast . Wendy plays on the radio and it's pretty cool to hear the Beach Boys while living out here. Its time to lock up the apartment and leave this crazy town. The car looks like a giant mess with all this music gear and we all look out of this world. Damian's wavy dreads and Lee's long blonde hair blows in the wind as we head out south bound down route 5. Old betsy is pure fire on these California roads. The Doors LA Woman comes on the radio as we drive past the Santa Fe Springs exit . We race some guy in a red ford mustang past the Buena Park exit. Lee hasn't seen his Mom in a year he says to us as we pull off the exit for Anaheim. We drive to the house which is almost in Garden Groove . Apparently the house is a giant 2-story house as are all these houses. Reminds me of the homes you see in the ET Movie or some movie set. "This a very rich area of the town, so we might get pulled over for your outta state plates bruh ".

Once we got there we most diffently look like we came from LA. The Once shiney white Buick Regal of Love is now a Dusty Dirty Done Dirt Cheap Car. We get out at Lee moms house and we all feel outta place. Lee walks up to the door and it's of course locked. Damain and I stand by the car waiting for the big wave. Larry rings the doorbell and waits. He curse's and starts to go to the back door when all off a sudden the Door flys open and it's his Sister. She's a stunning platinum blonde with long straight hair. I turn to Damain and say "ya bruh she looks pretty bad " . We both just laugh out loud. " Heys guys come on inside ".

We walk inside and are immediate told to take off our shoes. Also don't let the dog out and to park off the street or we might get a ticket. Lee's mom is friendly but warns us about her neighbors and the local security patrol for this area. No drinking and smoking unless your in the back yard. blah blah blah is all I hear its doesn't stop for about 20 minutes. Both Damain and myself can't stop looking at

Lee's sister. She's a little hippie girl but she's also kind of a preppy. Lees moms does real estate and is a million dollar seller.

Ha-y-n and myself head to the car to unload our gear. We pile it up in corner of the garage. Lee finally shows up and tells us that his mom doesn't want us to play cause she's fighting with her next door neighbor and he might call the cops on us. "Well that was a giant waste of fucking time bruh". We all sit there looking around at all over stuff everywhere. Lee's sister walk in and says " Hey moms not gonna be here all night you guys can play when she leaves ". Lee's sister turns my way .smiles and says me " So I heard your old enough to buy alcohol, cause me and friends would like you to pick up some Absolute Vodka " . She Smiles at me, than hands me $20 an says "Keep the Change".

The three of us drove to the local liquor store and bought some vodka and a case of budweisers. We have about 30 minutes of covers to play and than Its a free for all. We all talk about playing some Judas Priest or the Motorhead covers since we do it all the time at school. We get back to the house and there's a few cars already parked along the house. Lee's sister's boyfriend and his buddies are all here. We look outta place and these guys all look Cali cool. "You play guitar man, right on". "So your from LA .....Right On ". "You guys ever heard of Janes Addiction or Guns and Rose's " .That's the conversations I had with these guys for almost a solid ten minutes and then it was as if I wasn't there anymore cause nobody ever talked to me again. Damain and Lee got the same treatment, and we kinda sat at on one side of the yard and those guys stood on the other side. Somebody finally plugged in a radio and out blast Van Halens Pretty Woman.

More people arrive and the sun is going down . We need to set up the drums and get a sound check before it gets dark. We pull out Damain drums and setup in the corner. Lee and I can't find any electric outside where we are. We need to move the drums to the other side. Fuck me. Ha-Y-N picks up the drums and Carry them over to where the Radio is plugged in. Back and forth bullshit with these guys about playing.Were a AC/DC tribute band, and were gonna jam some songs. Nobody seems to be into us. This is getting worse. I setup my little amp and so does Lee. We start to get heckled cause the amps are smaller than the drum set. Some dude walked up and asked "So who's the singer " . Up to this point nobody ever asked us and I didn't really think about it. " You guys are a band doing ACDC without a singer, Right On man ". Damain says to him " Your gonna love it it's the craziest thing you've ever seen, just wait ".

I keep trying to tune up my guitar but the strings are all flat.

All these guys walk away and start smoking a joint. Lee and I setup our guitar pedals and sheet music. All of a sudden Damian starts to warm up and gets into a nice drum solo. Everybody is enjoying the jamming. For about 2 minutes Ha-y-n keeps the beat going and the echo off the walls of the house sound awesome. No Sooner was he done and the next door neighbor yells out " I'm calling the police" and slams his back door.

About ten minutes later the security officer pulls up to inform us there's a noise ordinance and that our 1st warning. We're all like " It's the 4th of July Dude ". Officer Mc'douche drives away in his white crappy fake cop car.

"You guys need to keep playing " says Larrys sister.

I pull out the bag of fireworks and tell these guys were gonna blow some shit up. These guys look at my firecrackers and bottle rockets and just start laughing. " Are these really fireworks cause this is some kiddie shit you get at truck stops ".

Once again I made friends and than I made no friends all in a night. I also haven't gotten stoned since we got here and I'm about to start drinking some beers. It gets later and later and the sun is down behind the clouds. The music is blasting, and we are all in our little areas drinking and smoking. Lee and I watch our guitars like hawks since everybody wants to play them. As people walk by they like to tap the cymbals which of couse is pissing off Damian. The radio is super loud and the cops haven't been back yet. its about 8:30 and were thinking it's time to play. Larry made a set list and we are starting with " Hells Bells. Dirty Deeds, Highway to Hell and Those About to Rock ". We play these songs at the jam room all the time. We are gonna kill this stage. This is our 1st show. We are so ready to rock and roll this hoochie coo. We walk over to the guitars and slide on those amps. Damians grabs those drums sticks and moves his drum set in closer. " Are you guys ready 1, 2, 3, 4 " crash goes the cymbals and without hesitation Lee starts to play those Hells Bells strings.

I come in with the heavy Malk chords and like clock work we both pick scrap back to the beginning. It was the fastest set of songs that I ever remember but it might have been the longest cause as each song played we had less and less time to watch the crazy antics. Dudes started moshing around and knocking over the lawn chairs. Somebody fell over the walkway and spilled there beer all over the place.

Lee sister was there and it looks like she was dancing and kinda head banging. But I think that when the security cops came back and where knocking at the door. "You guys have to stop NOW". "Either you keep the noise level down or were going to arrest somebody". We eventually walked down the street to a baseball field were we all watched the fireworks in the distance. Our once cold beers were all warm. We did it man. We played our first show and it was awesome. It was a quick set but it was a great set. We would later light fireworks in the street and everytime we saw cars lights we ran into the garage. The moon came out and the midnight air was crisp and clean and smelled very expensive to me there. Damian and Lee had the spare bedroom and I was given the couch downstairs. It was a real Loud and Proud event. I won't ever forget Anaheim and the nosy neighbors. The punk kids from Garden Grove and how cool we sounded on that back porch. This was an awesome show and I want to do it again every night of the week for the rest of my life. I really feel like we have something special here. We need a singer and I'm gonna make up some flyers for the GIT message board. We talk about the show and what kind of gear we need like bigger amps, spot lights and a van with the nick name Halen. I walk downstairs to my couch and grab one more beer . I get up and walk to the car to stare at the Moon one more time.

Its early sunday morning and this was why I left New Jersey a month ago. The road still haunts my adventurous self and I miss driving across the county.

I miss a lot of things that I used to always did. This moon makes me happy. I'm lucky to be alive and have these guys as friends. I'm really California dreaming and its not on a winter day.

June 6th, 7th 8th and 9th

I wake up and go to the print shop of broken dreams and make my little $10 a hr and try my best to not get dicked over by the boss/owner who hates me. I parked my car in the employee parking lot the other day. He didnt know it was mine and tried to get it towed. I mean really. I talk like I'm from New Jersey when I get mad sometimes. I act like I'm from New Jersey and thats what my license plates says on the fucking car. This owner knows I'm from New Jersey and thats why this dude is tick turd and I'm looking for another job with Sir Speedy print shop over in north Hollywood. I filled out the applications and all i need is an interview.

This stupid car all of a sudden isn't running right. Ever since we drove back from our gig last week. I don't know what's wrong with it. "Could be the gas" says my Mom who I talked too today. She is happy I'm out here doing some music and jamming. " Keep jamming Mark and play your little heart out " is she keeps telling me.

Life can be a real bitch sometimes. It's al[part of the good and bad things that happen in life. Some people will help you no matter what and some people like to snicker and poke fun of you. I always had the best of both worlds.This whole week has been just like that. Up and down and everything across the neck.

I got to see all our teachers perform after hours in class this week. It's the 6th week of fun and the teachers all jam after class with who ever stay and hangs out. A lot of teachers have private lesson after class. It pretty cool and it all sounds really wild when you hear people say "There's a secret show at the coffee show on Sunset at 11pm are you going". How can you say anything but yes and than no. I have to go home and practice and get up for work at 7 am I feel like I'm losing time out here and the more I look at the calendars and all the upcoming shows I'm wondering will I be here or will I leave and go back to New Jersey. As of right now school is super cool but the full time year long study is pretty damn awesome. My Sunday private lessons teacher kept bugging me to sign the paperwork for the full year course already. Lots of students are going for the full year course. I need to apply for student aid and give it a shot.

I went to ticket master and got my tickets for the Slayer concert in August at the Hollywood Palladium. So fucking cool man to have been able to do that. Lee and Damian like the riffs and all the screams, but they dont like the satanic words and its hidden meanings so they dont want to go. But we all might go to the Monster Of Rock concert with Metallica and Van Halen. There's so many shows going on it's hard to not get any sleep out here.

It's about 8:30am and its boiling inside our apartment. The Air filter must be clogged cause this ac unit is pushing out hot air. Damian and Larry call Maintenance, but he's outta town til the weekend. We bought some fans and try to watch tv but its to damn hot in this apartment right now. I was able to dig up loose change for a 6 pack of Coors beer and it helps with the heat. Larry and I have been working on our scales and riffs for the next week at school. We are always opening the MI/GIT books and sit there reading notes and figuring out the riffs and solos. We each play with and without headphones and it is all good to just practice any way we can sometimes. Lee's two hand tapping is getting amazing. I tell him "Dude your killing these notes". Yo Larry " I bet you didn't know this but Angus doesn't do two hand tapping in any of his solos ". I'm like dude what if " Eddy and Angus were on the same stage who would win ".

These guys all laugh as I do my impressions of our favorite teachers given lessons. Some teachers whip through these pages and other teachers just like to shred it in your face. I love this school and all the teachers all super cool. " Someday I'm gonna teach music here and my logo for all my guitar lessons is going to be a broken pick with broken drums sticks like a Jolly Roger ".

Chapter 4 - Finger Picking with Slide, Hold the Mayo

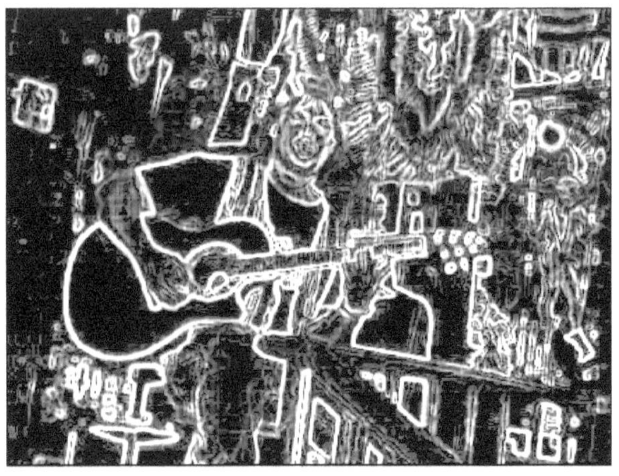

July 7th, 8th, 9th and 10th

The weather is amazing again these past few days here in Hollywood. Plans are forming every second of every minute and I can't keep up with the demand. GIT is getting super fast pace at school where we are going over everything from the past few weeks and amazing how much better I have become as a student, reading music is getting real easy and I'm able to understand theory more and the relative major and minor chords scales and substitutions. As a band we can rip through a set of ACDC songs pretty good and our back and forth guitar riffs are fun to do. I want to go over to Dee's and Tommy for a session. Now that the holiday is over we can all concentrate better on things say Mr Chas one of my favorite teachers at this school he tells it like it is, and he's a great guitarist. I really enjoy his class. All the class's are great Tonight is Monday and its Mr Chas for Chords and Rhythm and my man Mr Storming Norman Brown on ear training/sight reading. Dude is a mastermind of the fret board. Dude can lay it down on the guitar and he's version of

" Isn't she Lovely " by Stevie Wonder is amazing. I want to jam with him and Mr Chas after class sometime but as soon as school is over everybody rolls out like Faster Pussycat.

Tuesday was electric guitar and theory with shred master Mr Nick. Nicks band is playing next week at the world-famous Troubadour. The show is all ages and Mr Nick says we can get in free. I am going to that show for sure cause I want the spirit of Jim Morrison to take my lizard soul back to that desert highway in Death Valley. I can hear the clicking of the cowboy boots and the horses stomping around as a dual in the middle of street begins.

I woke up wensday and the car won't start but I was able to jump it and get to work fairly quickly. I hope I dont run outta gas cause I'm using quarters until I get paid again. Nobody is your Friend on Payday over here in the city where your Name is in Lights. I'm worried about the car these last couple of daze. The car is losing water and I'm constantly filling it up. I need to take it to a repair shop soon. Plus I'm up to like 5 tickets for parking on the wrong side of the street during " street sweeping " days. The money is wracking up and up and of course Lee's sister wants to party with us again. She wants to go to Universal Studio and see all the cool movie props. Plus its posted all over the city from one telephone pole to another about the " Monster of Rock concert with Van halen, Metallica, Kingdom Come, Kings X ".

Somebody even posted them over the Janes Addiction show. That's a big NO-NO to post over another bands flyer. Who ever did that is a real Howlie Boy Bruh. Dude I cant stop talking like I'm from Ha-Y-E These guys talking around me got me laughing with there little catch phase's. Last weekend I left work and hung out with Jose and his Sister. We left the south side and drove up to the observatory in the Hills of LA. It was a Full Moon and I was on fire that night with just doing something wild on a Friday night. The sky was filled with stars and we were all able to look through the telescope and see the aliens sleeping out on Uranus. I was busting jokes all night and since I was sipping on Tequila and Coke. We got super connected after all that when we left to go back to their house. I remember playing poker and falling asleep on the couch with my leather jacket.

I woke up and I was naked and my clothes where all over there living room floor. The place was super tidy and clean. I remember getting dressed and finding my wallet and keys. I walk down the hall and pushed open the door. Jose was snoring in his bed and so was his sister down the other hall. I left a note saying " Lets jam and party real soon ".

I walked to my car and it won't start. We must have left the doors open and the battery is dead.

I locked the door behind me and so I'm hung over and I dont know where the heck I am. I walk to the corner store buy some coffee and ask the cashier if he wants to make $10 and get me a jump start. He helps me out and doesn't even charge a single dollar. He was parked out back and basically drove over and jumped old Betsy. People in the south side of LA are pretty cool. I dont think that would have happened in NYC. I have met a lot of cool people out here like that. I've made some cool friends in the past 30 days. I drive back to Hollywood and pull into the garage on North Beechwood. I pull into the Villa and its almost all full with cars. Whoa thats a first I think to myself. I drag my hungover ass to the apartment and nobodys there. Huh ??? . A note on my guitar case reads " MALKS we went to Anaheim. Also look at the phone bill cause my Dad is pissed off at you ".

I look at the phone bill and it's a dew-zie . Its almost unbelievable but I know that word doesn't exist. $168.00. That's a lot of money and I'm looking at the numbers and its almost all me but Damian and Lee have some long Distance calls. As I break down the Phone bill I'm about $75.00 in the hole for calling my Mom and Dad along with calling my sweet girlfriend back home. She should have come out to Hollywood but her Dad told her if she leaves she can't come back home Ever. She's Missing all this crazy California lifestyle to cut hair and be a hair dresser. East coast stress is why I'm in the sunshine with palm trees and run way models Hahahahaha.

That what everybody back home thinks and its wonderful. I got another Sunday alone in Hollywood. I lock the doors and take off all my clothes. Click goes the radio knob and Ozzy's " Crazy Train " blasts across the living room. I grab my guitar and turn on the amp. I'm rocking out with my cock out and this is the best Sunday morning I've had in years. I take a shower and wonder what it would be like to go on tour and have to take a shower in a tour bus. Day in day out things go better with rock. So I turn up the radio and its sounds so good in this apartment. I wonder if were the only rockers to ever blast out music here. I can stretch my guitar chord to the kitchen and open the refrigerator and there's a two open beers and one unopened. HAHAHA I grab the unopened Beer and start to pound the table and salute the DJ who played this track and that band Autograph who recorded this hit song. I spend the rest of my Sunday hanging on the strip at the pizza joint and have met a girl there named Danielle but everybody calls her Dani. She works on the weekend answering the phone. She's very quiet and doesn't say too much. We smoked a little bit behind the kitchen by the dumpsters. She Likes my bike and asks me if we can go to her favorite beach in Venice. I tell her I have a car and we can go anywhere she wants to go. Dani tells me to stop over tomorrow and we can talk more cause she has to go back to work.

July 15th- 20th 1988

So much stress out here in the Hollywood Leo season. We are being slammed with lots of lessons and I'm being worked to death. I'm filling out a kazillion applications for jobs and I'm still getting nowhere out here in these streets.The Loud and Proud band is kinda getting bla bla with us always playing the same old songs. I have some cool riffs I want to jam and so does lee but we ant getting anything together when we jam at the apartment. The noise level is through the roof. I can't sleep with these guys up all night and than I'm supposed to wake up at 6am and roll out to work as if I'm super printer.

All I want to do is start a independent label and start recording my own songs. I have a bunch of great songs in my head I want to jam and all I get is the same old ACDC songs. I've been jamming to a lot of Slayer now that I have tickets for the show next month. Damian thinks it's all devil music it's not postive, and he really doesn't like there meaning. It's been a little bit of tension since we played our big show on the 4th of July

and now damians finding issues with everything and his dad isn't helping any of us enjoy the good times out here. Damians dad been calling the apartment to see who picks up the phone. He like to call and say things like " Hello this is Damian dad where is he " hahahah I laugh everytime he calls.

He told Damian to not let leave the phone out when I'm around. He is really pissed off that I'm here living at this apartment with these guys and wants me to pay the going rate to live in Hollywood. To bad that is not gonna happen while I'm still back in Black.

Chapter 5 - Dropped tunings, Pick scrapes and Whammy bars

July 20th - 30th 1988

Just like Johnny Winter says " Be careful with a fool ". We are a only a few days a way from the Monsters of Rock Concert here at the LA Colosseum. Van halen, Metallica, Scorpions and Dokken are the line up at this show and its going to be so rad. Ha-y-n and Lee crank out Metallica's

Kill'm all on cassette tape that I have on in the boom box in our living/recording studio. Its Sunday and thats my fun day to go for a nice bike early morning bike ride.

Its another blue sky morning and it's gonna be a hot for teacher day. Of course it hasn't rained and I love it here so much. The weather is amazing out here today. It's been a real struggle like a dog on a chain waiting to be unchained. Larry, Damian and Larry's sister Lisa all have tickets. I'm the last one and I keep telling them I might no go. I'm now working out a print shop in Burbank. A family run print shop and I like the fact that I'm not being yelled at when ever something goes wrong. I quit the other print shop job about 30 minutes after I got my Friday paycheck. I told the boss I'm giving you a to-day notice. He said to me with a mean face " you mean 2 weeks right " I said to him with a grin " I mean today notice ".

I had a huge smile on my face as I walked out that Santa Monica print shop. I also got into a little bit of fight with Jose there cause I told him I wanted to ask out his sister and he didnt like that idea at all. The Haynes family print shop treat me a lot better and there AB DICK 360 presss are a lot newer. If only the guys back in NJ could see me now haha ha hee hee.

So last weekend I went to the pizza joint and started talking it up to my favorite girl there named Dani. She told me she was in trouble in Hollywood and wanted to leave it. She also wasn't getting paid right and lost her tips. She told me to " Pick her up after work on Friday cause it's her last day ". This should be interesting and i wonder if she wants to start a band. She might be a killer lead vocalist for the Loud and Proud band.

So Friday comes around and I picked her up and we drove to the Venice beach for the evening. We walked the boardwalk toward muscle beach. We both walked the shoreline watching the sunset and we shared a kiss. Later that night she said she wanted to stay with me cause I made her feel safe. The operation mind crime was about to begin. She spent the night and met the guys in the band. I think they like her cause they dont stop asking her a ton of questions like " Do you have any sisters ".

The next day Dani asked me to take her to the Glendale area to her good friends house where some of her stuff was. We drove to her friends house and she knocked on the door. She walks in the house and she never came out. I knocked on the door after about 25 minutes sitting in the car waiting and this skinny dude opens the door and tells me that his name is Brad. He plays guitar as well and grabs his acoustic guitar to show me some chords. We jam back in forth and he's down with the metal scene. I ask him about Dani and tells me " She's upstairs with my Brother man, the've been a couple for a yr or so, and he kicked her out and now she's back - are you two together ". He and I jammed out and I smoke some of my herb with him. Then I fist bump'd him and started old Betsy up . I blasted the horn and spun rubber all the way back to Holly weird. I dont think I'll ever see that girl again but that dude was a really good guitar player so it all worked out.

A lot of fun in a short period of time and it ain't stopping anytime soon. We are celebrating each night with laughs beers and loud and proud rock and roll baby. I can't believe this month has been so action packed. This weeks mentor at the school was Joe Pass and was totally amazed at his playing style. What an amazing guitarist and of course he's from New Jersey so that's even better. School is getting pretty crazy as some of the teachers are being moved around to different classroom's. Plus some classmate's are already leaving town while new full time students are showing up and hanging out. The school is such a great place to be inspired and creative at. I sit on steps and jam while waiting for my private lessons to begin. My instructor keeps telling me to sign up for the full year course. She feels like I'm a perfect fit and all I need to do is keeping sight-reading daily and dont stop reading music. She tells me that her band is playing again at the coffee shop on sunset and to stop over and check them out. I tell her I will get the full time application fill out and she can help me fill it out. Her prerequisite will ensure me getting into the school. That such a great feeling and as I'm biking back home with my guitar strapped to my back I think I'm a lucky guy to have her as teacher. "California Sunshine Girl" plays in the background at the gas station as I pick up a 6 pack of beer and some clove cigarettes. The Monsters of Rock concert is tonight and I'm still without a ticket. I worked all week at the new job and they dont mind overtime so I'm working Saturday which is a big problem for all of us. plans change and feeling get hurt I guess. I really dont want to go to the show. I'm in need of some rest and sleeping at the apartment lately has been rough. We party and jam into the night and waking up is a real joke. Lee's sister Lisa was going to come over and spend the night and we would all go to the show early to see all the bands. Now that I'm working Saturday They are all going to Orange county for the night and I'll meet they over there.

I worked all day that Saturday drove back to the beach wood villa took a shower and drove over to the concert wear it was jammed packed with metal heads I parked old Betsy and walked around looking for any scalpers to sell me a ticket. I missed the Dokken show, the Scorpions show and the Metallica show.

Everybody was talking about Metallica's riot and how crazy it all was. I got a scalper to sell me a ticket for $20 and I went inside to catch Van Halen and find my buddy's. I had just seen Metallica the year before when they opened for Ozzy so its wasn't any surprise they had the place going crazy. I must have walked the entire stadium parking lot looking for the Loud and Proud crew buts its night time out and I see so many platinum blondes and dudes with black curly hair. VH plays in the back ground as I sneak around looking for any signs of these fools. I finally spot the three of them in a sea of dancing people on the second floor balcony. I sneak past security and get over to them where Ha-Y-N is super wasted dancing the night away.

I see Lee and his sister and that when Van Halen started to play " Love comes walking in ". I thought I was gonna dance with Lisa but her boyfriend was there. That's fair warning and he's all over her so I will have to admire her from far. " I saved one last doobie for us " and I pull out a thin white boy and light that bad boy up. That joint was the best I ever smoked in my life with my band mates while watching VH shred the stage. VH bowwed for the audience and ran off stage. " That was a killer concert bruh " .

Those guys left the concert with Lisa back to Orange county and I left with old betsy back to the lonesome Hollywood hills. The show was excellent and I only wish I could have picked up a shirt. I got back to the apartment about 1:00am and crashed on the couch.

Its 8:45 am and I am waking up to another sun shiny day here in the city of lost angels. I can't believe I ran into those guys but I'm also not surprised since I was on the look out the whole time. That's just to funny as I sit here drinking the last of Damains Kona coffee hahahah he's gonna be pissed off come tomorrow morning when he has to drink folgers again. hahahah.
Its Sunday so I will call my Mom and maybe call my girlfriend with my secret hidden spare phone I brought out from NJ. This is how I'm able to call jersey without using damains telephone. If only these guys knew. hahaha .
I want to head over to Dee's and Tommy's place to start a jam maybe even record some tracks. I want to go to the beach but I'm so tired from last night and I'm beat from all the walking. I'm just gonna take a shower and kick back in the ac and watch some tv while running up and down this fretboard playing these chromatic exercise's with major minor arpegios. I pull out my notes and my journals and start to write out all the crazy stuff that happened to me this month. May, June and July are gone daddy gone.
It seems like yesterday that I was stuck in Nebraska wondering if I would ever be able to make it to California. I could write a book about all the people place and things I've seen in the last 2 months and I've got another month to go so who knows except the shadow.
Oh man only one month left and than its on like Donkey Kong. The Clash " Should I stay or should I go " plays on the radio in the background. I light some incense and setup my BC Rich Guitar and this is where I become one

with this piece of wood with metal parts on it.

I start to jam along to the radio and it sounds so good. I love to jam along with radio and get lost in the music.

August aka Augmented 1st Thur 7th 1988

Look in my eyes what do you see is it a cult of personality. Its getting down to the wire with all this and that over here in Hollywood. The phone rings and I dont want to answer it cause it could be Ha-y-n's dad. I've already told my family back in NJ not to call me unless it's an emergency. Ha-Y-N's dad is being a real jerk to me and everyone else who dares to answers his phone line. He paid for it and I didnt and even though I did pay for it and thats why his son Damian is wearing them cowboy boots right now. We spent the other night fighting over the car which isn't doing to good. Its over heating everywhere I go so i'm not using it and I'm barely able to get to work. I have been talking to a staffing agency about working as a tradesmen printing for them. I was over at Dees and Tommys looking for a place to crash next month when these guys decide to go back to Hawaii. Angus and Phil want me to go to Hawaii with them and keep the Loud and Proud band going down there. They have a studio space and we can play anywhere cause Phil and Angus know everybody. My guitar instructor at GIT wants me to go full time to school with her and stay until i get my degree in music. So many different things to do right now and my shoulder hurts probably from sleeping on the living room floor next to the couch. Phil's dad called to tell him and Angus that " I'm sending some killer bud, be careful ". Damian tells us "Bruh this Maui herb is so good you might see Jesus and not go to that Slayer concert ". I'm quick to point out how

I was right about Metallica and I'm right about Slayer plus I've already bought a ticket for the Slayer concert and its going to be insane. It go to be at the Hollywood Palladium. I feel like the only guy at the school who is into thrash and punk but I know its not true. The pranks have been pretty damn good as of late. I was able to watch Lee drink his entire beer without noticing the cigarette in it that damian toss in it while we played 5 card poker the other night. I went to a yard sale the other day and bought a bunch of magazines. The guy gave me the entire box for like $5.00. I got some Guitar Player, national geographic, time and a few porn magazines where thrown in. I tore out some centerfolds and placed them in Damians drum pads for school. He opened up his drum pad in his PIT class and all these nudie pics came falling out. Hahahaha It's all fun and games around these parts. We have pranking each other like this for the past few weeks. Lots of people are at the school this week getting ready for the full time class's. Most of the class's are getting smaller as we keep getting closer to our last few weeks of school. The teachers are always having after class jams with all of us. They are stopping by our rehearsal sessions and listening to everyone jams and songs. I have been trying to get the recording sessions with Dee and Tommy going and it's been started that this weekend we are to come over. We can record anything we want and Dee will mix all the parts for us . A goal of mine was to get a demo tape over to Capitol Records before we leave for Hawaii. I have been really thinking about leaving and I'm not ready at all. I'm losing another job and my cars need some major work. I need to pay rent and that phone bill. I am in a jam and all I want to do is jam so it makes no sense but i'm smoking some sense so there ya have it folks.

So after our electric guitar class our teacher decide to inform us that his band was playing at the troubadour and if we showed them our GIT pass's we would get into the show for half price. He told us that the more students from MI showed up he was gonna play louder than any other guitarist ever. I've only heard what everybody else heard and we all said yes Nick. So the Loud and Proud guys got all dressed up for a friday night rock concert and showed up to the spot where Mr Mojo Rising, Elton and Janis once played. We filled up Betsy with gas and water headed down to the place that is the best. I bought us a bottle of Jack and put it in my leather jacket. Phils cowboy boots were super cool looking. Lee's denim jacket with ACDC patch's was killer. We drive up behind the club and park where we could. We were laughing the whole time trying to find this place. As we walk to the front door the Bouncer looked us up and down stood up from his bar stool and said " I need ID from all three of you guys ". "We're with the band" said Lee and from that moment the bouncer hated us. the GIT badges didnt work at all for us either. I was 19, and they were only 18 with three different state id's. He looks at everything and than waves in a local. He says this isn't gonna work guys I can't accept this card cause he couldn't read the date on it.

He was being a real jerk for no reason, but he could. He waved in another bunch of locals as he kept fucking around with us. You guys have $10 each I'll let you in tonight but you still can't drink here. We agree and walked inside to the most famous bar in LA.

We watched a bunch of great bands who played some covers and than came out Nicks Band, and they started playing this bluesy Texas style rock. It was a super bad ass and so different from all the rest of the bands. I always like the blues and nobody else was doing it so it sounded fantastic to hear it. We would later roadie all the gear for Nicks band and than watched Lee get back stage into the green room with the bands where a bunch of strippers had there way with him. Larry never told us what happened up there but the smile on his face said it all that night. We drove home and crashed with our blue suede shoes on .

August/Augmented 8th 1988

Today is a magical day so I was told because today is the Lions Gate Portal to another dimension for all us humans in the positive world. Vibes are higher today and will be until the 1st full moon of the month which will be very soon I hope. I have written all my thoughts and intentions in the great notebook. I hope that everything I have asked for comes true. I think it will and thats the power of love and positively. In other news you can't use Lee tells me that his sister wants to go to Universal studios next week and that we can all get to see all these cool movie sets. So it has to get done before we all leave for the big island. I got a phone call from Jose the other night and he and his sister want to take me to Tijuana for the weekend. They of course have family down there we can stay with. We talk about my new job " Did I tell you that I'm working for another print shop and its for a few more dollars and is on the east side of LA off Galvez street for a pretty cool print shop". They print dirty magazines and want ad papers for a bunch of adult theme clients if you get my drift. I can't tell you who and what might be printed today Butt if you ever seen playboy or penthouse you might understand better. It's a tough job butt somebody has to print it. I tell Jose I cant make it for the adventure down south butt maybe next time.

Big blue and white fluffy clouds fill the skyline today. It's been boiling hot out and it hasn't rained again. I really Like LA but I really Love Hollywood. I can't believe it's going to be over in less than a month. My mind floats to the desert roads of Nevada and Arizona. I can't wait to hit the road again. I wonder if that Dad and his Daughter that I stopped to help made it home safe. Maybe This time I'll go to the Grand Canyon and jam on my guitar.

Chapter 6 - Harmonic Minors and Major 7ths

Augmented 10th thru 15th 1988

The radio is on our favorite station 105.5 the KNAC and its jamming the sweet sounds of " Jesus is Alright " by the Doobie Bros and its feel so good to be here in this apartment. It's been a wild week of work , school, concerts, movie sets and us making killer breakfast burrito's and hues ranceros with guacamole vaquero hold the mayo. hahaha.

" Bruh you looked possessed brah maybe you should not be around that devil music Malks ". This is all I kept hearing from these guys at school and at the apartment. Its so hot and so smoggy in this city of lost angels. A killer kinda day to have as a single guy. The smell of incense fills the air. The morning is slipping toward high noon and I have a list of Things to do a mile long. The lists and list and lists of minute by minute goals and dreams is nowhere to be found today and I'm ok with it. Work is going well and its pretty funny to be printing inserts for the adult classifieds.

GIT School is great and we have only a few weeks of sessions with these teachers. We are all on a first name basis and most of us have seen each other shows either at school or around town. The Loud and Proud guys showed up to see Lee's guitar instructor band play some hot blues and we got half-way there and the car broke down in the Middle of Sunset ave. Old betsy wasn't having it and she over heated about a car length from the Intersection. " I think we blow a headgasket " . It was a major issue for about 45 minutes while we sat there with a car filled with drum cymbals and guitars. Lots of cursing happened that night and we all said a lot of true blue dirty dog shit talk. Who started it wasn't even an issue. But I think that when that head gasket blow up so did ours. It took us about 3 hours to get old Betsy back to our beechwood villa. It was the best of nights and it was the worst. We didnt talk for days to each other. Were all friends now and have made peace so thats pretty Rad. It was all Betsy's fault but it was the Karma we needed to get all of us to work together and make this band stronger and become the road crew .
I sit here with my ears still ringing from the past 2 days of what is going to be remembered as 1 of the coolest

concerts I ever seen. Finally get to see Slayer jam fucking Friday night in H-Wood and

It was a Major event that caused the city to send the riot police. I was lucky enough to bike over to the HW Palladium and walk in no problem with my cool ass Slayer shirt I bought back in NYC. I think Danzig opened the show and it was badass. When Slayer came on the place went super crazy like always. The crowd pushed all over and I eventually got all the way to the font stage. I'm looking at these guys and than I get punched in the back of the head. I get picked up and now iIm crowd surfing when I feel somebody grab my leg. Security grabbed my leg and dragged me into there no access zone and threw me out the fire exit door onto the city street. I was pissed off and I kicked that door about six hundred and sixty-six times. I wasn't the only one and a few more people got tossed out the door. I finally went up front and the police where there in riot gear defending the entrance which was filled with broken glass and trash. I watched the street get lite up overhead as spotlights from the Helicopters told us to " Evacuate the Premises Immediately ".

I left to head home and almost got jump by some cops in a squad car who tried to run me over but I bike'd my ass off into on coming traffic and ditched them.

Its Saturday and only have to work a half day at the print shop. So I stopped over at my favorite tower record store to see about the upcomming Slayer show in Riverside Ca. I buy 2 tickets with the plans to sell the other ticket for double to get my money back from last nights bullshit in HW. I leave about 12:30pm to the record store and the guy working says " It's a pretty far ride man ". So I head out west La and I fade away from the city. The radio station plays "Cute" by Zappa and I'm rolling down the Freeway. I picked up a bottle of Jack and a 6 pack of modelo for the show tonight and unloaded anything that can get stolen out the car in case I have to park in bad area of town.

I get to the DE ANZA theater in Riverside and its closed as is almost everything else in this lonesome western town.

I park behind the loading dock and walk around the place. I sit in my car and wait for somebody to show up.

I'm playing my acoustic in the front seat drinking a beer when I see this bus pulling to the parking lot.

It pulls up right in front of my car and stops. The door opens up and out steps the bus driver. He walks toward the back of the bus and opens up some compartment doors. Three blonde haired girls walked out the bus doors along with some guy. That's when I started to see the next group of guys walking down those steps and it was the band Slayer. The guy with the girls walks over and says " hey can you let us in to the building yet ".

I step out the door of the car and shake the guys hand and I say " Hi what's your Name " To the girl on the right with leather dress on. Dude looks at me and says " Are you with the Local 33 Stagehands ". I smile and laugh at him and say " Nah Brah I'm with The band Loud and Proud Local union 007 ". He was not impressed and neither were these ladys. I quickly walked up to the band and said " Yo you guys were fucking killer last night in hollywood ".

I told them all about my experience seeing them and they where really cool, and they laughed. I thanked them for talking to me and shook there hands and watched them get back into the tour bus. Later that night I sold my extra ticket and watched Slayer put on an amazing show. It was one of the loudest shows I had ever heard. I partied with the stage crew and got invited on the tour bus. I got home about 3:am and I think I'd really like to join the local stagehands union. I think i would be good at staging and lighting. Made it back to Hollywood and I slept like a little angel of death that night.

Monday Augmented 15th 1988

I wake up with a crick in my neck and it's from all that head banging I did this past weekend. I think i'm only gonna do half a day and try to get to school with these guys on time. Ya know what " Fuck it Malks " is the motto today and so I just called in sick. I'm taking the day off. Lee says " lets go to this place I heard of its called " Guitar Center brah". I heard Eddy Van Halen hand prints are in the front like the Walk of Fame ". We all shit, shower and shave as fast as we could . We drop $10 bucks in the gas tank at our favorite shell gas station and hit the freeway. The Car is working a little better but I still smell antifreeze and all I do is watch the water temp gauge everywhere I drive. It times to get another car or maybe a motorcycle. It's also time to get a new guitar and amp setup. It's time to find another job and maybe today's the day.

Once these guys knew I wasn't going to work and we were going for a car ride it was like old times again. We were laughing and joking about everything. It seemed like a million years ago that the three of us first met and got stoned and jammed. Mondays traffic wasn't to bad and it took us not to long to get there and it was fucking rad. As soon as we got there we stated to talk about all the music gear we wanted and heard about. " We need a 4track recorder and some real microphones ". " Brah I need a better flight case for these cymbals , mine looks like its from 1950 " . " Dude , I just want some guitar pics and maybe a shirt ". We walked around that store and play every cool looking guitar they had. I walk over to a killer looking Gold Top Gibsen Les Paul on sale for only $2700.00 once played by the original Kiss guitarist. All the salesmen were hawking us the first 5 minutes. Now they are forced to help other customers and thats cool cause Lee's playing on a bad ass $1200.00 Gibsen Les Paul SG with red velvet lined guitar case. " Dude this is why Angus can play the licks that he does ". He hands me the guitar and instantly I feel like Angus Young. This guitar is so bad ass and its so smooth to play for a left-handed guitar. " I always forget your a lefty dude ". Lee was a bad ass now with the guitar. he could play right-handed ok , but he was wonderful left-handed and so i was always impressed with his mindset and control to learn guitar around everybody else who was right-handed. Eventually we would get 3 applications and fill them out in the store with the hopes all three of us would work there. I'm sure all 3 of those pieces of paper were thrown away by the guy who told us he was attending the Grove school of music and that our school didn't match the same criteria of credits for a real degree in music in California. All three of us agreed that " dude was a Howlie boy " and we didnt want to work around him and his snooty fox attitude. I think the best guitar I got to play on was this jet black Grover Jackson Charvel strat style with floyd rose tremolo system. I felt like I was Randy Rhoads or Steve Vai at any moment on that fret board. I was shredding up and down that fret board like it was the easy breezy Sunday morning. I also had the pleasure of playing a Sold Wood BC Rich 10 string Bitch guitar and I'm totally blown away at the workmanship of the guitar. Every single inch of this store is rad and I want to come back here every weekend for test drives. We spent about 3 hrs and spent about $40 hahahah and as we left all our favorites and loves behind we drove to another guitar shop and this one was even more rad.

We drove out that parking lot and turned left on Pica street and headed to the coast to see the ocean side for what might be the last time for the three of us and old Betsy. The weather is on point with trippy looking clouds in the horizon. Without any real knowledge of its existence we drove into Santa Monica and spotted another cool music store. We park old Betsy and enter this very cool and streamlined shop. These 2 guys instantly welcome us into there establishment and talked to us instantly about what we like about Music. " Do you guys like Rickenbacker cause we are an authorize dealers " Than instantly hand Lee a black Rickenbacker and says " Tom Petty plays the same one on stage ". The 5 of us are all telling stories and talking about this musical life we live. We are walking around checking out all these guitars and than I spot this killer looking blue Ric and I ask to play it. We Play everything in this store and these guys love it. " You guys know that Brain Jones of the Rolling Stones was a was huge Ric player., He drowned in a swimming pool not to far from here ". Ha-Y-N is not really into this and there not a big drum selection, so he's looking kinda bored until the store owner says to him " You wanna play a signed Geddy Lee Ric ". The guy grabs a dark blue Ric off the wall and hands it to him and says " Geddy Lee of Rush was here in the store not to long ago to fix his personal bass and we loaned him a few for his show that weekend he just so happened to signed this one ". Big smile's came on Ha-y-n's face as did all of us.

As we drove back from that store to our Monday class's we had probably played over a 1 million dollars in gear today.

We drove back to the villa and spent the rest of our time changing guitar strings and thinking about all the cool stuff we just played. We were all inspired to jam and play some shows and go on tour. Talks about recording a Dee's place was back on the table of events that need to be done before schools out in less than 30 days. 30 days til its all over for us Summer session guys and its all about doing as much as possible.Tonight Lessons are gonna be Chords and Scales with Mr Chas and than Sight Reading with Mr Stormin Norman. Both classs will go hand in hand as Chas will teach us about 7ths and 9ths chord melody lines and than Mr Norman will teach how that translate to the theory and sight-reading of these concepts. It's a nice breakdown and its very in depth information. Alot of us are now recording the class session with mini tape recorders. I need to get one and start recording everything myself. I really like recording music and a ton of ideas for songs. The Loud and Proud demo tape needs to get made but also the jam sessions with Dee. I have only 2 days to play the song Black Bird with Mr Jamie during our acoustic guitar class. I was playing this song for the past few weeks and I'm ready to rock this song out. I cant wait to have a real jam with one of my favorite teachers at GIT in front of everybody. I want to make up some flyers for it and post it all over HW.

August 10th 1988

I have been working overtime at work to make as much money as possible for every single thing i want to do before the end of the month. I am also in the middle of signing up for the full year at MI/GIT. The Loud and Proud guys are all on board with going to Dee's house to record our 1st 4 song demo tape. I have been writing lyrics but I'm still not sure if i should sing. I wrote the following lyrics" I drove my car across this nation to be with you girl and rock your station with a pick and an amp and this broken guitar I hope we go very far cause were .... Loud and Proud " . I hope to add more lyrics before the weekend come along. We decided to play just 1 instrumental and 3 songs.We need to create a logo, and we need to design our demo and get some cassette tapes. I asked my boss if I could make some business cards with the used ink and paper we are throwing away, and he said " Ok Mark whatever you need , Just remember me if you guys become famous ".

Chapter 7 - Easter Bunnies Get Drunk At Easter

Augmented 15th 1988

" Big Girls Don't Cry " sings Frankie, old no blues eyes. Every once in a blue moon I am able to find another station to play and today it's the golden oldies station. I love 1950's music and all the harmonies with zero guitar solos. hahaha. Tonight at the school is a special instructor class with students to perform. But I think I'm just going to grab some beers and hang out with Dee and Tommy and get ready for the recording session. I have my amp and guitar stuff over there right now. I did a quick jam with Tommy the other night while Dee worked out the microphone placement. I just love how serious everybody become when the tape rolls. Dee has a red light bulb in one table lamp and a black light in another floor lamp. He switch's one each one to let us know when we are recording and when to jam and have fun. He has a bed sheet over the kitchen door and one over the hallway in to the bedrooms to close off any sound from the outside world. He knows how to get a nice clear sound by dropping all the low end of the equalizer during playback so it isn't so heavy sounding for our double tracking. Lots of cool tricks with the mic and amps. Dee knows about recording demos from working as a dj in the radio business. He loves to tell stories of how the Ramones recorded there 1st album and how the Clash recorded their albums. He knows a lot about music and it is really is fun to be around him during all this engineering madness.

Augmented 16th, 17th, 18th 1988
" Just got paid today and I got a pocket full of change " plays loud and proudly on the Knack radio this morning
" Bruh Ant that the truth today " says Lee who is starting to pack up some of his clothes. Damian and Him are getting ready for another refreshing swim at the pool today. I am going to do a run through on the car before I drop it off at the auto shop for a head gasket. For only $250 buck a roo's the car will be better than new. The mechanic working on my car says if I want to sell the car after its fixed they would buy it. Seems my car is kinda in demand out here in the LA area. Ha-Y-N and Lee think I should sell the car and buy a plane ticket to Maui.
I have been using the bike and I'm kinda outta shape and I pulled out my hip from biking too much in the past couple

of days. Old age at 19 sucks Brah. Its only 2 weeks until graduation and I'm feeling really weird. Its super nice out today with no rain in sight again. The clouds are fluffy and the sky is blue. I might bike down to Dee's and listen to our recording from this past weekend.The recording session was long and hot as hell in that non air-conditioned apartment. We recorded on four radio shack cassette tapes and now Dee is mixing those tapes down to a complete songs and eventually a 4 song demo for the Loud and Proud band. I was able to make up some business cards and J cards for the cassette tapes. The Loud and Proud logo isn't on it cause we couldn't find anybody who can draw what we wanted So I used some bold typesetting from the graphics department at work to design it and it looks great. You can read it from 50ft away. The Inserts are pretty funny with our thanks to our Mom's, Dad's, all our Instructors and friends at GIT-BIT-PIT. Hahahaha

Excitement is all around us musicians today and for so many great reasons must be a full moon rising.

Today is our Sin-day to just chill out and get some laundry done and maybe go to our private lessons or go to the beach or church for one last time.

" One last Time " should be the name of our 1st album cause that all where saying around the apartment. Lee and Ha-Y-N are hilarious this morning and now I know why. " Malks I hope your ready for the most amazing thing ever ". We all walk over to the kitchen table, and he pulls out from his duffel bag a manila envelope from Waikiki, Oahu . " Brah back up cause when you fall over I dont want you to hurt your head ". Ha-Y-N cuts open the package and inside is a nice happy birthday car and a rolled up t-shirt that unfolded to another wrapped present. We all had happy faces as Damian ripped open that sweet smelling bright lime green herbal medicine. " Whoa , Bruh look at that super killer Maui Wowwie ". To this day I have never seen anything like it. Damains dad sent him a care package that is going to make all of us happy happy happy.

We made some Kona coffee and packed up a bowl. The entire room smelled like funky funk. We were eating cookies and laughing at each other when we heard three loud knocks on the door. We all stood still looking at each other. Again 3 loud thumps on the door. We all stood in place looking at the door. Then it stop and we just start laughing. Lee walked to the door and opened it up. He looked around and than he said " OH Hello, ok dude thanks " than slammed the door while holding some piece of paper. It read Your apartment need to be checked by maintenance, and we must be out no later than 5:00pm August 31, 1988 Thanks MGMT . " Wait - What the fuck are we gonna do Brah , Thats not right brah ". Damian and Lee start to argue so here we go again around here. As they start to argue over the who what where and how's I'm reminded of my 1st days here at MI/GIT.

I thought I'd be living in my car over in Santa Monica with views of the ocean each morning. I'm so glad I made plans to stay at Vegas and Dee's Place for the rest of the month. I grab my GIT book and start to read my jazz lessons for today's private lessons. We are going over the 2-5-1 progression using the C-D-E- Minor 7th /9th (13th) with 7b5 Dominants / Altered Dominants. It's a lot of deep theory with practical applications toward jazz compositions. I am just starting to like all this smoky time jazz jams. It's a kind of music that only gets better with practice. I'm learning about time signatures that I have never been open to with these Jersey rock and roll eardrums. I only seem to hear jazz when I'm at School or heading over to the coffee shop where it seems all the MI/GIT staff hang and play a lot at.

I have been asked to show up and play but my jazz skills are just not there. I didnt move to Hollywood to be in a jazz band even though I wanted to learn all everything and stuff about it. I feel like my style is more rock and so all I want to do is turn up the distortion pedal , step on that wah wah pedal and shred that fret board.

Chapter 8 - WWHWWWH is WYSIWYG

Augmented 16th & 17th 1988

Time flies when your having fun Brah. Your in this world and than your not in this world. We are in the last few music sessions here at Musicians Institute. There is so much going on and we only have a couple of weeks to go over all the latest material and the old lessons. We are down to a few students in ours class's. All of us are jammin making demo's to sell our songs to either get a record deal or get a gig for something to pay all these bills that I owe them aka Bill Odem and the All Stars might be a new Band to join as well. We are Excited to jam again and record more songs at Dee's place. he has all the cool tricks to make us sound great. I called my mom and wished her well as i'm about to see her soon and party once again along with the rest of the family. We all want to see our family. Musicians institute is now our mainline family. Last weekend we recorded at Dees place and it was Radical. Dee's is very experienced in making the recording project sound perfect . He uses the Red White and Blue recording method. The white and blue lights are for jamming and having a jam/practice time. The red light is for recording only. The blankets over the windows and door ways makes for sound proofing. Dee has recorded several bands in Pittsburgh, and he gonna hook it up for these demos for our hook up at Capitol Records. The Loud and Proud band recorded a 4 song ACDC tribute demo with " Hells Bells , Dirty Deeds, TNT and Highway to Hell ". The other recordings were with Tommy, Dee and Me playing some Blues Jam. We played and recorded into the night and drank all the Capt Morgan an Cokes that night. Dee and I snuck up to the roof and drank some beers on the roof of the building. It was so cool to hang out on top of the streets of Hollywood looking down into the south side of LA. We had already spent the entire week talking about playing and so we spent the entire night recording onto that stupid tape deck. The microphone fell over for no reason that night. The overdubs didnt work the 1st time we did it and had to do it all over. The recording process is amazing and it sucks all in half a second. You can press record and play the greatest version of a song and than listen back to the worst sounding shit you ever heard. But we got Dee and all these tapes sound great so I can't wait for the mix tape and our artwork for the cover, so we can drop them off with our hook up at Capitol records. We only have 4 weeks and I dont think I'm going to Hawaii and I dont think I'm staying in holly weird.

August 20th, 21st 1988

24 hrs to go and I Wanna be Sedated plays on the radio. " Hello kids we are Loud and Proud and my name is Malks this is my brother Angus and his name is Phil Mc Phillerson " hahahahah. It never gets old saying this dumb shit to all the newbies here at MI/GIT. We have so few students in our class's this week that we are all in the same room to learn the last week of lessons. We are learning about playing styles like Reggae, ska and flamingo methods. Larry and I are now in the same class and thats kinda fun. We get to learn to off each other to play these back forth jams. We are very lucky to get along and also kinda be known for playing in a band. Dee has told several people that we've been recording demo and that were having a giant party at his apartment this weekend and " Every weekend until school ends ". So It's exciting to know we have a couple of shows lined up. Dee's recording studio has been been I find myself hanging out at after school. Life is changing and the full moon has taught me once again what's important and what's a load of crap. It only another 2 weeks and its all over for us coming to this

killer school. We are packing everyday and than we repack again and again. The couch and kitchen table along with chairs will be gone in another week. I Have cleaned out the Malks wardrobe closet and its 100% good to go. Everything I own is back in the back seat of the car or in the trunk. The car is running great and I keep it all wax'd and shiny for the big ride home. I'm excited to see my friends and family back home but this has become home and dont want to leave.

Its super nice out today and I'm so trying to do everything I can at work and school. I have given an offer to work as security and possibly need to be armed but I'll make a lot of money. I went to the interview, and they want me to sign up for class's and take the state background test for my gun permit. It way too much to think about as i'm being hounded by the MI/GIT administrators to complete my full time student paper work. I also haven't made any plans to change my drivers license or plates. Its just goes on and on and it all has nothing to do playing guitar and writing song for a tour. We have been just sponge as much time from our teachers about the who's and what's of the music business as well as how to play that killer riff. " It's all smoke and mirror's " It a favorite saying our mentors tell us when the answers are really left up to us in life. It seems like we are masters of the music game but as soon as we hit the street it becomes a " Dog eat dog world out there ".

I was telling myself " I'm a lucky guy " and than I found a couple of self-help books that have made really question this life and who I am as a person. I really need to write my own book about music but I feel like I don't have enough time.

I still think about that little girl and her dad stuck on the side of the road while I was enroute to California. I hope they are ok. I'm glad I took a chance to help them out. Someday that might be me on the side of the road with my daughter. I think about Dani and her long blonde hair and I hope she found love with that guy. I can't complain but sometimes I still do and thats when I can at least make that phone call to my mom at the TRW credit union where she's been working at for the past 20 yrs and ask her for some advice.

Oh my God this is the craziest news I've heard since I've been out here. So the other night I get a call out to my girlfriend back in NJ and she told me that " Your buddy's Pat and Gus are living somewhere near a beach in California ". I told her to drive to Ausgutos's mom house right now to get me a telephone number and an address. she still pissed that Larry's sister answered the phone and said " I'm sorry Malks not here he's taking a long hot shower probadly thinking of you ".
I can't believe these guys are out here. I drove out to see Jose at the print shop in Santa Monica. He and I drove down to Venice beach and than went to Huntington to go people watching and be on the look out for my high school buddy's. Gus is a jaw dropping guitarist and Pat is a killer guitarist/singer. If we could get these guys to come jam with us at the studio with the Loud and Proud band we would have a 5 piece band and that would be the most radical shit ever . I might even sign us up for another open stage show on Friday night at MI/GIT. The last time I jammed with those guys was last summer. Like wowwie man that a radical thought. It's a " Blast of the Past " to

think about where I am now and where I was just a few years ago. I drove all over the place and all I got was stoned. Jose told me to stop over when ever to hang out and of course we should go to TJ for the weekend. I didnt tell him I was leaving town in a few weeks. I should have but I didnt want to make a big deal about. He has been a cool friend to me and I probably should not have tried to kiss his sister that night. But we were all drinking, laughing, playing strip poker and thats what sometimes happens in the big city. My life is so crazy right now with all this news from all over the place. I hope Jose and his sister get outta that apartment complex and get a house cause that place is kinda ruff. I drive off and think to myself that I probably won't ever see him or this side of LA again. I really want to drive back to the beach and look for those Subliminal Seduction band mates who won the Battle of the Bands back at my High School. Hahahahaha. I will keep looking and hoping to run into these wild and crazy Jersey guys.

Chapter 9 - Turn up the Radio

August 24th, 25th, 26th 1988

Hooray the new demo tapes are here, and they look so Radical Brah. 10 cassette tapes with j-cards with our correct names and phone numbers. 4 songs of great rock and roll to be handed out to all these studio bigwigs here in the land of nuts and honey. As we handle our tapes as if they are gold the three of us each get 3 copies and the last one is a toss up. Larrys sister wants a signed copy and my teacher Mr Jamie wants a copy. the guy at our favorite gas station even wants a copy and tells us we can sell them at his store. We finally asked the gas station guy " what's your name Brah " " My name is Mohammad " so of course we now call him Mohammad Ali cause he can " float like a butterfly and sell like bee ". He asks us " What do you think about that Tyson fight , it only lasted 30 seconds ". We all walk out and say the same thing " That dude is awesome i'm gonna miss not seeing him anymore. We are listening to our demo tape in the car and we all think the same thing as it plays through old Betsy's speakers is how " I fucked up that beginning part and I wish we could redo it " also " I forgot to add that little part in the solo " we need another take cause " this demo sucks we should get our money back Brah ". hahahaha. This is the music business at its finest. We busted our ass to play and record and now the demo tape sounds like crap. We drive back to the house, and we shake it off. " I'm gonna drive down to see my security guard friend and as him to drop off our tape to the AR Department ".

I picked the red tape and grabbed my back pack and headed down to Capitol records. I didnt see my Buddy there hanging out protecting the rich and famous. So I did a quick bike ride though the streets of Holly-hood. The bike almost knows where i'm going and I drive past Musicians Institute and head over to the pizza shop. Looking inside for that long blonde hair girl. I pass my fav tattoo shop where I got my name with an anarchy symbol inked. I bike past the corner where we all stood there talking to some dude who said that he was an actor and chased after a car who took a picture of him. I drove past the place where i got this strange hoagie sandwich one night it was called Subway. I went down to see Mohammad Ali at the Gas Station and get a tall boy PBR for dollar but he wasn't working. I drove the blue Schwinn back to Capitol Records and there was man. " My man fifty grand how you been Brah ". I hand him my cassette tape and tell him all about it. He asks me if I went to that Interview for the Security job. I talked about Life Liberty and Pursuit of Happiness. " I'll drop off your tape and if you get rich you better not forgot me ". I feel like this could be the start of something great. Big Mike the security guy has always been cool with me and I hope we get a call back. I head back to the apartment to tell those guys the good news but there not there. So I start to sweep up the kitchen floor and clean up the bathroom. I really like pick sweeping and floor sweeping.

Its 12:33 am and i'm popping open a can beer just like Mr Mojo Rising. The Doors song LA Woman blasts out this boombox and in the background is this empty hollow sounding apartment. All the furniture is in the living room now and all of it is now so clean and shiny. The place isn't a loud and proud recording studio anymore. It just looks like a giant white wall dorm room. Damian and Larry have been using Colgate tooth paste to hide all the holes in the walls. I am in charge of also cleaning the Ac unit filters and the bathroom tub of course. Larry is in charge of cleaning the kitchen and oven. Damien is in charge with telling the landlord he can come in to inspect the rooms next week. I really wish we didnt take down all our posters and fun flags of freedom. The place looks like we dont belong here and it smells like a hospitol room. It has a very uncool feeling here now and thats why I like going over to Dee's and Vegas place. Dee has decided to stay in LA for a little while longer. Tommy going back to Vegas at the end of the month. Dee has put the room up for rent at $250 a month and that why he wants to have a party this weekend. Dee thinks i should move in and we could start teaching music or recording music demo for bands from scjhool. I really like how Dee's mind thinks about music all the time. I thank him for all his help for mixing our demo's. I didnt pay Dee a single dollar for any of his help and he didnt want any money. Yet he still wants to jam more music and keep releasing new music demos for artists. I did buy a bottle of Jack and a bottle of Jose a few times along with the fine herb and wacky beers. The only money we spent was on those radio shack cassette tapes. In a big country jams " Ana Ng " on the radio. We stand in the kitchen watching the world walk by though that kitchen window facing the parking lot. "The boulevard of broken dreams is right outside our window". Tommy has headphones on and is practicing his rudiments for next weeks lessons at PIT.

Dee's kitchen is always a mess but it has that family feel that make me feel safe at home. This side of HW is cooler than where I'm at right now. " I haven't met a single neighbor in the apartment building where us loud and proud guys live but I have heard them kick on the walls when the music is to loud ". Dee says to me " It's a different kind of people man, you live where its rich, were in the heart of city " chuckle's come form Tommy over in the living room. We clang some beers and hail an " amen to that brother ". Tommy shows me a map of Vegas and tells me I'm more than welcome to drive out with him at the end of the month. " I got a complete garage filled with equipment and its sound proof ". There's a lot of work in Vegas and the best thing is that its only 5 hrs back to LA. Tommy and Dee got me thinking about a new way of living in this rocking band. " You could work at a Vegas casino and record music in the studio on the weekends in

LA ". Whoop whoop thats the sound of the Police and its on like Donkey Kong right now in this parking lot. " COPS ARE INTHE PARKING LOT " screams Dee to us. " Time to lock the front door " says Tommy as he walks over to a dresser and slides it across the doorway. We are all ganged up next to the window watching the cops run though the parking lot to chase somebody on a bike. It's gonna be a hot minute to leave this place. Four cop cars pull up and block off the entrance to Cherokee street. " This sucks were stuck here until this shit cools down ". Dee and I grab another beer outta the fridge and say " Fuck It Lets Jam ". We walk over to our favorite spots in the living room. I grab my amp outta the closet and plug in dudes black Bass guitar. Tommy grabs his drum sticks and gets behind the drums and starts to hit them super loud. Dee sets up the microphone and starts to flip a cassette into the tape deck. I crank up my amp and start to play " Breaking the Law ". Within a minute we are jumping around singing and jamming super loud. We played for about an hour. The cops finally left and I was able to finally go back to the Beach wood Villa to do the whole thing all over with Damien and Larry. The jams never really stopped as Larry played the Acoustic , Damien played his Pads and I played the BC Rich guitar without an amp. I am really gonna miss living this rock and roll life with these crazy fools 24-7-365 !

Chaptor 10 Dont Fret It, Just Shred It

Aug 27th, 28th 1988

My mind is mush and I need a cup of coffee with a shot of espresso to hold back the Whiskey that wants to come back up and haunt me. Last night was a lot of fun as the 5 of us got together for another night of hot jams and killer laughs. A few people showed up to Dee's Saturday Night GIT-BIT-PIT Party. We played a bunch and than watched a bunch of other people who i didnt know jam out. Everybody who showed up is a absolute monster on their instrument. I just love that big sounding distorted rock songs with that heavy metal band vibe. That low end bass in dropped D is so bad to the bone. I think Dee found somebody who might want to rent out the spare room. Dee's idea to record bands is going to be exactly what this under ground music scene needs. Some off us dont have the money for all the big studios and with so many bands taking up the studio's at school and though out the city. He's going to make a killing engineering demo's and mix tapes. Dee and I spent time hanging out on the roof again talking about the music business. Dee says " We need to make our own record label and create tours for bands ". " We can do anything if we keep it a positive thing for the music scene and not just rip off people and steal there songs ". As Dee talks I am trying to figure out why there's a number 33 on this beer bottle. We agree to never let some major label run our life and steal all our songs. We also made a pack to start a record label. " 33 yrs from now we will come back here and throw a celebration party "." Dude I'll be a 50 yr old man in 33 yrs and I might not make it, so we gotta live this life as fast as we can cause it's can be over in the blink of an eye ". " We have only one more week until we all have to go out on our own and i'm not gonna ever give up until I'm dead cause music means freedom ".

I wake up this morning and turn on the radio to hear Dio singing Mob Rules on the worlds greatest station Knac 105.5 . I'm about to get some beans together of this Kona coffee and boil up a small pot for what might be the last good cup of morning joe . I wont ever forget our coffee drinking and how it made us all calm. I am all alone in this empty cold apartment room and of course I get naked as a jay bird and decide to take a shower . It is a delay reverb echo chamber here at the beechwood villa. Ha-Y-n and Ha-Larry-us are having the last Sunday at the swimming pool or as Ha-y-n says " a refreshing swim". So I decide to prank them and i put on my beach shorts and run down to the pool area and jumped in the pool. My shorts came off in the water so I ran out naked dripping wet all the way back to apartment room laughing my ass off down the hallways the whole time. All I heard was " Malks Don't Do It Brah ". But I just did it and I think the 2 old ladies who were sitting at the table might call the cops on us butt who cares cause were out of here in less than a week.

These west coast guys are gonna hate me but they need a good laugh from this jersey guy one last time hahahahahaha.

Chapter 11 Odd Time Signatures and Dirty Notes

August 23 1988

Its a sunny hot Tuesday and Jesus is just all right by me because " Jesus is my friend " sings on our radio in our crazy echo chamber of an apartment. The movers came early and took both beds, the kitchen table, the black and white TV and chairs along with the living room table and the dresser. The only thing in here is us and its pretty damn crazy to see nothing. I took some penthouse mags from the print shop and taped some of the centerfold to our bath room walls and back of our front door, I even tape a nude pic on the inside door of the sink . The movers also took the microwave. hahahahaha we have another week, and we need to be out so what the hell are we gonna do. Larry bought the tape player over from his moms house, so they didnt take that. I found us a few crates at the laundry mat, and we found an old suit case to make a table. We sit in the living were the ac blow's out cold air, and we talk about tomorrow, next week, next month and the next couple of years. All we have is our GIT papers guitar player magazines and guitars." Yo malks brah you coming to Waikiki with us you know we got you with everything " . he syas " There's a ton of print shops to work at ". I just laugh and I always say yes while shaking my head no .

We are sipping maddog 20/20 and share'n pbrs again like it was our 1st week together. " Brah keep the phone plugged in case Capitol records calls us ".

School at GIT has been very cool with lots of great jams with a mellow vibe afterwards on how it was all done. Our instructors tell us how to get out here and play, find a bunch of like minded musicians and start a band and write songs. While the summer is ending the GIT crew keeps jamming in packs after class and it is fun to turn it up and get loud. Some of us are just drifters now and we are the Hollywood rats that hang again trying to get some fresh cheese. The teachers all tell us how much we are always a part of the GIT family for life. We are all on this fretboard of life playing our hearts out trying to make a little better than the next guy. Don't ever give up on your dreams and play as much as you can morning noon and night. " Positive thoughts brings positive things in music is a gift and you all have it " and dont forget to "Share the gift of music with other far and wide ". My classs were so special to all of us . The last few days we all leave class and hugged or high five each other goodbye. We went to a after session party ever single night this week with a late nite show at the clubs. We talked like pros and our teachers helped us keep the beats together until our big celebration and ceremony next week on the big stage at MI this Friday night. Saturday is Loud and Proud last show at Dee's recording studio and than these guys are leaving. I think im gonna stay and hang out with Dee and Vegas for the next week. I can make another $500 bucks at work and than roll out.

This last week of MI/GIT, Hollywood and jamming with the Band is hard for me to really concentrate.
So many great bands and musicians are here jamming and I didn't get but a second to see and hear it all. I Only got a few seconds to hold on to it. I got to touch it and it was amazing. I tried and I made it all work out ok. But time is running out and I am trying to not think about it. I slowly ride my bike for the last time through the old dirty side walks i thought were so fresh when i first explored this land called Callytown. The sun is setting and the dash board of this old Buick is showing the dust. The radio plays some old Louis Armstrong " you go to my head ". I really dont think anybody is ever gonna believe any of this ever happened. I stare at our demo tape and i wonder about everything that could ever happen but probably won't cause in 3 days our phone number won't be available

anymore. I should have put my number from New Jersey on it. Damn this rock and roll lifestyle. Haaahahahahaha. I open up the glove box and there is the little blue children bible I found in the kitchen a few weeks ago. It's nice to see it and read it right now as i'm sitting in my car in Santa Monica. " Some day I will live here and I'll be a teacher at MI ". the sky is turning red white and blue. The Saegulls are flying all over the beach. I also want to go fishing but t best I leave it alone in the trunk. I think about taking a walk but it's better to just sit here and watch the world fade away. Im a Lucky Guy to be able see this and it's been a very special summer. It NEVER rained here in Hollywood the whole Summer. Ha ha ha hah staying alive staying alive. Tomorrow we are supposed to get instructions on our full time class schedule at school. I have been told about a killer house party in Beverly Hills. The Loud and Proud Band has been asked to perform at a bunch of places for parties but after this weekend were unavailable. I am gonna miss this place and all these bad ass dudes I've met in the past few weeks. This has been a really cool place to learn about music and show the world what you got. I dont think i could have done this any other way. I have no regrets and no remorse. The only problem I have is that I still dont know " the way to San Jose ". Parking gas and parking cars is a magnet for many if you dont know the way.

Chapter 12 Dirty Reeds Bought Dirt Cheap

August 24 1988

It was a very very very hot day at the print shop. I'm so tired and I'm fighting to stay awake. No rest for the wicked they say . I'll sleep when I die. We are in the last few jam sessions and the last of the very last nights at the GIT laboratory for all us scientific explorers of the fret board. I keep thinking of everything we learned and all the great moments here. Teaching guitar is better than printing letterheads and envelopes.

I almost fell asleep on the hour long traffic jam in the car while driving home from work this afternoon.

I am so excited to see who shows up tonight for class. We are constantly asking for arpeggio lessons or sweep picking tricks in this key or that chord group. We all have our demo tapes ready in case we meet someone in the business and needs a late night session player. Meeting and greeting people is where its at in this flashy town. Speaking of meeting and greeting dont forget the good eating. I hope Larry and his sister come over for our " Last Meal " together. I have some last minute pranks for that situation later. I'm gonna miss that girl and all her upper middle class high society life.

I also hope this weekend is as nice as it was all week here in holly wierd. The weather has been hot during the day and cool at night.

I want to get some new clothes for the party this weekend in Beverly Hills at Lita's house. Her and her boyfriend are hosting the event and some of our teachers will be there so this is gonna be awesome.

I get home about 5:00 pm and came home to some dumb ass drama as Phil and Angus were very upset that the wall in the hallway of our apartment got damaged while the movers were there the other morning. The moving company has stated it might be there fault but nobody called so they are not responsible for the damages. Damian is freaking out that his dad might have to pay a late fee. I tried to help them with a quick drywall repair kit at the hardware store but they were going to get it fixed by the maintenance guy for $100 bucks. " You Still kinda owe us this last week for rent Malks so just pay $75 for the past 3 days and that we'll cover the cost for the room repair ". I still shake my head but I handed over $75 bucks, so we could leave without having that bad karma on us. " Dee said we can stay at their place until the end of the month " Ya Brah were going to Larrys mom place until friday's ceremonies and than we'll party with you guys all weekend". We dropped off our keys on the kitchen counter. We shook hands and I left that situation as fast as I could.

I drove old betsy out the bat cave one last time. I was pissed and I was sad. Those guys took off with Lisa and I just drove around the block in my car. what the fuck just happened. I went to work and when i get home we are now unable to get back into our apartment that I just paid up on. This is total crap but I'm not gonna listen to any of this and just go back there and do my business. I didnt get to even take a shower when I was sitting there. I just can't believe it all. What the hell just happened. I drove back to the apartment after thinking fuck it I have a spare key hidden in the garage just in case. I drive inside the parking garage and park. I get out and walk with my back pack to our " Old " apartment room 13 F, and open the door and it was like i was home. I dropped my stuff on the floor and started to take off my clothes to take a quick shower with no sun glass's no radio blasting and no black light. I Took the longest shower of my life that day. It felt great to think of everything I had just done in the past 100 days. I still have a million more times. I placed my spare key back in the garage and drove off thinking that if I ever need to come back i know where the key is.

Now I'm driving to GIT for the last of our jam sessions to laugh and learn more about the music, the theory and the business, Plus that lawyer who will take half for the rest of your life. School always makes me feel good when I'm here and the class is only the 10 of us. The teachers are going over every single lesson we ever had. Page after page. non-stop. The sight-reading is amazing and the talking about how it all works is rad. I am in awe of all of it. I keep being asked " Are you staying for the full year Man " . I never known what to tell them.

August 25, 1988

It's Thursday night and it was a hot one today at the print shop for all of us pressmen. I was able to make some business cards for " Dees Recording Studio " and I was able to see some new nude calendars that we are printing for a high end magazine company. I can't name any names but let me tell ya you know who i'm talking about. Last night was going to be our last class for all the summer session students. But like always these guys have figured out to do 1 last showcase for the few who have decided to show up and learn. We meet at the rehearsal area aka the Jam room and watch as the teachers put on a spectacular jam out while having students plug in to an amp and jam along in real time. There was a ton of jazz fusion mixed in with super fast classical speed runs, we had blues artists ripping the neck with 2 hand tappers laying the fret board to shame. Everybody was so alive as they past the guitar cable back and forth. I remember sitting in there thinking about my jams with Jamie playing Black Bird in front of the class live on stage. I thought about my night on stage for the high school variety show plating " You Really Got Me ". I remember the ultimate lesson when playing live on stage is to " NEVER STOP PLAYING "

Even if everybody else stops . When they finally handed me the guitar cord I almost froze still in front of everybody. I truly wasnt thinking of anything that was going on. I was somewhere else. I remember thinking of doing stuff that I hadn't seen anybody do yet. I did a massive pick scrap and pull out my slide and started ripping some sweet high notes. I played all kinds of scales and arpeggios and than handed the cord to this guy named Darrel who just shredded the guitar. Later that night Darrel and I talked about Dee's studio and he wanted to hang out there. He also needed a ride to the airport on Sunday. He wasn't going to stay for the full time session either. I brought him over to Dee's house, and he already new Vegas from another jam session so everything worked out. He said he lived not to far away from MI/GIT and was selling off his gear to make extra cash before traveling back to Chicago.

" If you ever in the windy city look me up man I know a lot of cool people there ".

The last class of MI/GIT happened and I met another cool like minded musician. He even smoked the herb and like to drink Rolling Rocks. I wish we could have jammed more than just once. I think thats what this whole experience has taught me. I am so grateful for all these cool cats who came here to jam. Not everyone is kind here in LA and I almost thought I wasn't gonna make it. I'm a lucky guy and everyday that I've been here has kinda taught me that. I can't believe I did this whole trip from NJ to CA. It's been a wild and wacky colorful pipe dream.

August 26th 1988

I worked from 7:00am until 4:30pm and the boss paid me in cash. I told those print shop guys it was nice working them and running that printing press. The owner told me if it doesnt work out back home I can always come back to LA and work for him . I'm really gonna miss this tiny little whole in the wall shop. I bet I could work here for the rest of my life if i really wanted to. Its not a bad job and the pay was ok. I would have never eaten out of a food truck if i wasnt here. I also got to hang out in Skid Row and see a different side to this city. I can't wait to tell everybody back home what i did here. Nobody is going to belive a single word I tell them.

I drove over to our old place on beechwood to take another sneak peak of it all and a " refreshing " shower . So i pull up and park the car but when I showed up to our apartment there was a bunch of painters inside the place so I left and walked around the building one last time. I left my key in the garage again except this time I won't be back for a while. It seems like I'm in a dream walking arounf this place. I keep hearing my name and I want to walk around but it doesnt feel the same. I feel like a stranger over here now.

Old betsy started up and we peeled out that garage one last time. I flipped off the Hollywood sign and drove to Dee's place. I took a slow walk to the apartment and i'm nervous about tonight ceremonies at school and all the people who will be there to get there certificates. There is so much to do before we get there and yet I dont know where tio begin.

It's 6:00pm and finally we are all here and I am still kinda nervous for all of us. The loud and proud band is getting ready to party and jam. The whole thing is coming to a big end with the band and we never got a call back from Capitol records.

We are all meeting up at Vegas and Dee's apartment for pre show jam and than a toast to all the good times. We have all pick our favorite outfits to wear with our acceptance speech's and the envelope's please. The winner for best prank on guitar goes to Malks for change'n all of Larry's guitar strings to all the same string. hahahahha.

I'm gonna miss this guy and his left-handed SG Angus Young guitar. Its 6:30 pm, and we are all walking down to the main entrance for Musicians Institute. Dee, Vegas, Angus, Phil and Malks are looking good in our rock t-shirts and jeans. Brown bags of beers while passing the douche from coast to coast. Were checking into the school and there has to be about a hundred or so students waiting around the stage area. All the staff and teachers are present and shaking hands. its very official looking and everybody is dressed up in suits and ties. The teachers have there fave guitars on stage to the far left with the center stage to meet Mr Pat Hicks and Mr Bruce Buckingham for our Certificates. I remember shaken a lot of hands. Lots of hugs goodbye and dont forget-me-nots. There a huge party tonight at another friend of our from class and it go to be open to only MI Alumni. " You guys are always be our family, and we well always be yours " they said. Each one of them teachers were great. We all received our and honers and left to go out 1 last time in LA and party like its 1999. We are all about to move out this weekend. The Loud and Proud guys took off for that after party in old

Betsy. She drove us there no problem. When we showed up the place was on high alert and I remember we had to jump the fence and have Larry open the gate to let us in. We got up to the party and it was super crazy with each room filled with people who are all drinking. We meet up with our class mates and had a toast of champagne with them. The music was pumping and the swimming pools was filled with people. We looked out of place or should I say we looked poor and so nobody talked to us . We left within 30 minutes of getting there laughing at how my car was parked next to a Porsche and a Mercedes Benz.

The rest of the night was all of us yelling and screaming out the window of old betsy until we got to Dee's place where we blasted the music and drank the rest of the beers making those 1-800 calls to Jose Cuervo.

September 3, 1988

" Were Has all the Good times Gone " plays over the kitchen radio while the 5 of us come back to life after last nights crazy after parties. We are to play our special last set of jams tonight " the last saturday night party for us in LA ". We are not up to playing and nobody wants to eat or drink right now. We are repacking all our stuff and check our bags into the cars and trucks for the haul across country. I'm kinda excited to be heading back to New Jersey to teach the world about GIT BIT and PIT. I've got a million ideas and I want to start recording as soon as I get a another band together.

It's been a radical adventure out west but nothing lasts to long in life and you have to make a change for better or for worse.

Its about 6:00pm and we are all very tired but we play some poker in the kitchen drinking dirty tap water and whiskey shots. Dee and I are the only one drinking beers and doing shots still . Ha-y-n and Larry argue over the time they need to leave for the airport tomorrow " Brah The taxi service was suppose to pick us up at the beechwood apartment and now where on Cherokee street ".

I remember being asked a million questions that night like " Yo Malks my family has a nice place in Vegas and my band needs a guitar player so you need to come to Las Vegas next week " and " Dude if you come through Pittsburgh you better call me " YO MALKS " You Need to come to the big island and jam on top of the volcanoes Brah " Yo Malks, Yo Malks, Yo Malks, Yo, Yo, Yo !

I fell asleep laughing at all of it at about 3:00 am .

Sept 4th 1988

In 24 hrs I would have left Hollywood Ca for Las Vegas and I spent a week there jamming with Tommy. We meet the Dallas Cowboys Cheerleaders in one of those casinos's. We went to every casino on the strip . We even had the same black jack dealer as in the movie Rain Man. I remember giving Tommy my custom cut off denim jacket with the band Exodus painted on the back.

I washed my car at the local car wash and old betsy is shining like a million bucks. I should have drove back on route 70 but i decided to take route 80 home. It poured rain as soon as I got into Arizona and it never stopped.

I drove through the night and it still rained when I woke up. 4 days in a row it rained and so I drove to Chicago where it rained the whole time there. I tried to call Darryl when I was there but the phone number was disconnected.

I spent a few days there busking for tips sleeping in my car. I would eventually get back to New Jersey and start all over again. Of course find a new band and jam was the main thing on my mind. A blues band, a cover tune band and another rock band. Maybe I'll start a jazz fusion band and a county band. I should play acoustic cover songs in coffee house's on Sunday mornings. I need to start singing more and buy a 4 track recorder. I wish I had bought that jet black BC Rich guitar at the pawn shop.

All I know is that I'm not wasting time no more and I'm gonna jam every day and twice a day in the summer in honer of my time in Hollywood.

The rest is history and of course like they say on the big screen

"That's All Folks ".